P9-CFD-431

More advance praise for *Baby on Board:*

"Finally a book that brings to light all the challenges of the modern mom with practical and inspirational advice for dealing with the changes of becoming a mother. *Baby on Board* will be on our best picks list for 2007!"

—Shannon DiPadova, mother of two, founder and president, DueMaternity.com

"After 30 years of nurturing new mothers, we know the demands of new parenthood are unexpectedly overwhelming and we welcome this resource to help moms-to-be plan for their transition to motherhood. *Baby on Board* goes right to the heart of the matter and helps a woman trust her instincts."

—Corky Harvey, RN, MS, CLC, and Wendy Haldeman, RN, MN, CLC, mothers, lactation consultants, and owners of The Pump Station, Santa Monica/Hollywood

"I certainly struggled, and I think so many mothers do, with becoming a mother and staying in contact with my creative, 'adult' self. It is so very important to give mothers the tools and permission you are given with this inspiring, practical book. Thank you!"

—Jennifer Louden, mother of one, author of *The Life Organizer* and *The Pregnant Woman's Comfort Book*

"Hooray for *Baby on Board*! Joelle and Amy understand that taking care of yourself is the first step in being a good mother."

—Stacy Denney, mother of two, owner of Barefoot & Pregnant, author of *Spa Mama* and *Fit Mama*

"Thank you for writing this book! I've been having so many questions about what I would be like as a mother or if I have what it takes to be a mother. Your book addresses all of my fears squarely on the head!! It helped me move from my 'mommy tailspins' to real actions that will bring my best to motherhood."

—Vanessa Birch, hoping-to-be a mother, owner of Communications Savvy

"*Baby on Board* addresses the missing piece for so many women in preparing for the births of their babies—looking carefully and consciously at what they truly need and want to be extraordinary mothers."

—Karni Seymour-Brown, mother of two, midwife, and owner of Sunrise Birthing Center

"I felt like I had my own personal coach and support team as I read *Baby on Board*. Someone to challenge my thinking and push me to look at what I want and take action BEFORE the baby arrives!"

—Debra Gomes, mother of one and soon to be two, owner of Note by Note Children's Music Studio

"The *Baby on Board* process made a HUGE difference in preparing for our second child. It brought my husband and me closer to each other, created the foundation for a great start, and now keeps us focused on what we really want for our whole family."

—Cynthia Salitsky, mother of two, Director R&D Communications, AstraZeneca

"Having become a mother myself just 10 months ago, my one piece of advice to new mothers I meet is to 'stop reading all those books and just *be* a mother!' This book is the exception. What we need most is to step into our own motherhood, learn to rely on our instincts, and become the parent we really want to be. *Baby on Board* is an amazing guide to doing just that . . . so grab a cup of tea and dive in."

—Tina Forsyth, mother of one, author of *Money, Meaning, and Beyond*

"*Baby on Board*'s insights and exercises are invaluable to any woman trying to define who she is and, more importantly, who she would like to be. Amy and Joelle have gathered a wonderful collection of inspiring real-life stories from moms and moms-to-be. Even those wary of the self-help section will find plenty of down-to-earth tips and advice inside."

—Katherine Tom, senior editor, Yahoo Travel

"You cannot possibly imagine or predict what kind of mother you are going to be until the day you welcome your little one into the world. The best possible preparation for happy, healthy parenting is to be a well-adjusted woman who knows herself and understands her values. Joelle and Amy have provided moms-to-be with a toolkit to guide them through this journey."

—Evelyn So, mother of one, president, Evelyn So Consulting Services

"I wish that Joelle and Amy had written this book 12 years ago before I had the first of my 3 children. *Baby on Board* is an essential guide to any expectant mother. It is like having a loving, wise and experienced friend at your fingertips at all times."

—Terry Curtin, mother of three, CEO/Creative Director, Intralink

Baby

ON

Board

Baby

ON

Board

Becoming a Mother Without Losing Yourself—
A Guide for Moms-to-Be

JOELLE JAY

AND

AMY KOVARICK

American Management Association
New York ◆ Atlanta ◆ Brussels ◆ Chicago ◆ Mexico City ◆ San Francisco
Shanghai ◆ Tokyo ◆ Toronto ◆ Washington, D.C.

Special discounts on bulk quantities of AMACOM books are
available to corporations, professional associations, and other
organizations. For details, contact Special Sales Department,
AMACOM, a division of American Management Association, 1601
Broadway, New York, NY 10019.
Tel: 212-903-8316. Fax: 212-903-8083.
E-mail: specialsls@amanet.org
Website: www.amacombooks.org/go/specialsales
To view all AMACOM titles go to: www.amacombooks.org

This publication is designed to provide accurate and authoritative information
in regard to the subject matter covered. It is sold with the understanding that
the publisher is not engaged in rendering legal, accounting, or other
professional service. If legal advice or other expert assistance is required, the
services of a competent professional person should be sought.

This publication is designed to provide information of a general nature and is designed for
educational purposes only. If you have any concerns about your health or the health of
your baby, you should always consult with a physician or healthcare professional.

Library of Congress Cataloging-in-Publication Data

Jay, Joelle Kristin.
    Baby on board : becoming a mother without losing yourself : a guide for moms-to-be / Joelle Jay
and Amy Kovarick.
        p. cm.

    ISBN-10: 0-8144-0907-5 (pbk.)
    ISBN-13: 978-0-8144-0907-7 (pbk.)
    1. Motherhood. 2. Mothers—Psychology. 3. Mothers—Conduct of life. 4. Self-realization in
women. I. Kovarick, Amy, 1965– II. Title.

    HQ759.J324 2007
    646.70085'2—dc22

                                                                                            2007000390

© 2007 Joelle Jay, Ph.D., and Amy Kovarick
All rights reserved.
Printed in the United States of America.

This publication may not be reproduced, stored in a retrieval system, or
transmitted in whole or in part, in any form or by any means, electronic,
mechanical, photocopying, recording, or otherwise, without the prior written
permission of AMACOM, a division of American Management Association,
1601 Broadway, New York, NY 10019.

Printing number

10 9 8 7 6 5 4 3 2 1

This book is dedicated to Tim, my beloved and supportive husband,
Jackson, who was the inspiration for the book,
and Morgan Adam, who played at my feet as I wrote it.

Joelle

I dedicate all my efforts and the results to every woman
who believes she doesn't deserve it all.

Amy

CONTENTS

FOREWORD

From the moment a woman knows she is pregnant, her routine ways of thinking, planning, eating, and sleeping are disrupted. Especially with the first child, a woman loses herself in daydreams about being a mother and what her baby will be like. She bounces between thinking how her life won't have to change *that* much to making baby-focused plans that completely disregard her present life and direction. While every mother loses parts of herself in the transition to motherhood, *Baby on Board! Becoming a Mother Without Losing Yourself* offers insight to help the reader stay connected and true to what is most important in her life.

In our present culture, more time is spent on preparing mothers for the day they are in labor than for the transition to motherhood that will follow. Many new mothers lament that they wish more time had been spent preparing for the longer and profoundly life-changing postpartum transition. Many childbirth educators argue that mothers aren't ready to hear about, or prepare for, the postpartum transition while they are pregnant. They will just have to wait and sort it out later. But later is too late.

Much of the literature available to new parents is focused on labor, birth, physical recovery after birth, and baby care. As someone who has worked with thousands of new mothers, I know first-hand how important it is to prepare for the changes of new motherhood. Being aware of, and planning for, normal postpartum changes can help mothers—and their families—adjust more readily. This is the first book I have encountered that brings a comprehensive approach to preparing psychologically and logistically for motherhood.

Baby on Board has a clear message: Every expectant mother is creating two lives—her new baby's and her own as a mother. Joelle and Amy believe that taking the time to go through this introspective planning process intentionally might bring mothers closer to their actual goal, which is to maintain their bearings even when chaos reigns.

This book is a thoughtful woman's companion to preparing for the practical and emotional changes in the first year of motherhood. The exercises outlined in this book will continue to be a reference and guide as a woman matures psychologically and socially as a new mother.

Pam England
Author, *Birthing From Within*
January 6, 2007
Albuquerque, New Mexico

A LETTER TO OUR READERS

When we started writing *Baby on Board*, the media was full of scary stories of new motherhood—stories of women desperately trying to juggle their lives, abandoning hard-won careers or missing out on their babies' lives, and generally starting to buckle under the pressure.

We set out to rewrite the stories of motherhood for our generation.

What we found was that it is up to every woman to rewrite her own story.

It is our vision that as women we will figure out how to have it all—not by *doing* it all, but by understanding what our "all" is: our unique, personal, one-of-a-kind way of living that takes into account everything that matters to us—and allowing others to do the same. Enough of women arguing over how a mother should live her life. It's time for women to come together and create a world where we honor each other, no matter how different our choices might be.

You, the women who are reading this book, are our inspiration. We know it takes courage to blaze a new trail. Every woman who steps out into a new life widens the path for the women who follow her. When you declare what you really want, you give another woman a voice.

We hope you will join us in our vision and use your transition into motherhood to live your full potential. It serves no one for you to hide your light under a barrel. If we had done that, we never would have written this book.

Please share your story with us. We want to know your experience of becoming a mother without losing yourself.

We look forward to hearing from you, and we wish you all the best.

Joelle and Amy

Write to us at stories@empoweredmotherhood.com.

ACKNOWLEDGMENTS

They say it takes a village to raise a child. It also takes a village to write a book. We would like to thank everyone who helped us reach our dream.

To our husbands, we give our deepest thanks and love. We could write this book because you have been by our sides, supporting us through early mornings, late nights, and the creation of this book. You fill our hearts! Thank you, Mike and Tim.

To our parents, Fritz and Evelyn Grupe and Frank and Susan Kovarick, we give our gratitude. Thank you for being the kind of parents we want to be for our children.

To our babies Jackson, Morgan Adam, and Matthew, as well as Layla, Fina, and Meli, we give our wishes for lives of fulfillment, balance, and confidence. What we write in this book for new mothers, we also want for you.

To our special family supporters, especially Jan and Logan, we thank you for every bit of editing, inspiration, and baby tending.

To our agent, publicist, and publisher, we extend our deepest appreciation! Sharlene Martin, our agent, you believed in us from the very beginning and took our idea into the world. Adrienne Biggs, our publicist, you rock! Stan Wakefield, Christina Parisi, Barry Richardson, Erika Spelman, Kama Timbrell, and the whole staff at AMACOM, you cared for our book as much as we do and made us feel involved and important throughout the process. Thank you for still believing that books can change the world. And special thanks to Stan for being a gentleman and professional and to Christina for giving so freely and generously. We also thank Walsh & Associates and Kathy Whittier for a wonderful job.

To our readers, clients, contributors, partners, and every mother we know, we owe great credit! You spoke from the heart as experienced mothers, new mothers, and mothers-to-be. You are our inspiration everyday. This book is filled with your stories, emotions, and advice. We could not have created this book without you. Special thanks to Beth, Debra, Evelyn, Fabienne, Gretchen, Joelle H., Karen, Katherine, Kelly, Kolmi, Kristen, Kristie B., Leslie, Lis, Linda, Lydia, Rena, Sabrina, Sarah, Susan, Sydney, and Vanessa.

To the organizers of the San Francisco Writers Conference and the Coaches Training Institute, we honor your support in shaping us as writers and coaches. You do good work.

We thank God for giving us the chance to be mothers and that we live in a time and place when mothers can also run companies, own their own businesses, choose to work or not to work, be professional, be ourselves, and speak our minds. We hope that our book will somehow contribute to the betterment of an already incredible life for every woman who reads it.

INTRODUCTION: CREATING YOUR LIFE

"You can't have relationships with other people until you give birth to yourself."

Sonia Sanchez

When you found out you were pregnant, you knew you were creating a life. But did you actually think about *creating a life*? Not just your baby's life, but *your* new life? You know things are going to change with a baby, but have you really stopped to consider what those changes mean for you?

Who do you want to be as a mother? What will make your first year as a mom ideal? What will you need to feel fulfilled in your new role, as well as in the rest of your life? Taking the time to contemplate these questions will enable you to take charge of your transition into motherhood—to define and create your new life on your terms.

There is plenty of advice for expecting moms—sometimes *too* much—on everything from stretch marks to strollers. Books, magazines, websites, your mother, your mother-in-law, your friends, and even strangers are eager to tell you what to do. They all think you should do things their way because it worked for them.

We think you should do things *your* way. We believe you have your own answers, or at least the ability to find them. Only you know what's truly right for you. We've designed this book to help you release your innate knowledge, wisdom, and insight in creating your new life as a woman who is also a mother.

Becoming a Mother Without Losing Yourself

With this book, you give birth to your life as a mother. You think beyond the baby shower and the birthing room and design your new life to reflect what you value, what you believe, and who you intend to be. We refer to this book and our step-by-step process as *Becoming a Mother*. Your journey through this book starts with exploration and ends with celebration!

- You **explore** and **imagine** your ideal first year as a woman and mother, creating a personal vision for you and your family.
- You **reflect** on what is most important to you. You **clarify** what you believe about motherhood, developing a foundation that will serve as a guide for your new life.
- You **declare** what you want for your first year, capturing it all in a concrete prioritized list.
- You **plan** changes for your time, money, and space while working through the challenges that arise.
- You **commit** and **take action**, putting your new life into place before your baby arrives.
- You **celebrate**, acknowledging how extraordinary you are.

Each chapter encourages a combination of thinking and doing with examples, exercises, and anecdotes to help you design your life ahead. The process is flexible—you can work by yourself, with your husband or partner, or with other moms-to-be. You choose how little or how much to do and with whom to do it. The tools in this book are available for you now as you enter motherhood, as well as for the rest of your life.

> *"In my process, I wrote down what I value—independence, growth, self-awareness, and passion. These are the qualities I want to hold onto as I become a mother. I designed my ideal first year as a giant learning opportunity—with a plan to dive into child development books and classes, have some time every week to be by myself and reflect, get a new digital camera, somehow find a part-time job based on my photography, and go away for a weekend with Ron to celebrate our five-year anniversary. It is so cool to write down what I want!"* —FRANNIE, 7 MONTHS PREGNANT

Throughout the book, you will meet other women who have generously contributed their thoughts and experiences of becoming a mother. They represent different walks of life, career paths, family arrangements, financial circumstances, cultural backgrounds, and opinions. We have changed their names and specific details out of respect for their privacy. Their ideas, plans, and actions range from the lofty to the practical. You will read about an expecting mother vowing to honor her integrity, another letting go of her fear, and others who are taking a promotion, leaving a ten-year career, finishing home repairs, adding a home office, and preparing for life with a baby in dozens of other ways. We hope you embrace your process with the same enthusiasm and commitment.

> ### WELCOME!
>
> Different women will read this book at different times in their lives. For the sake of clarity, we wrote for the expecting mom, but we also invite new moms, experienced moms, and even sometime-in-the-future moms to enjoy the process of designing their lives.
>
> **All women are welcome!** Whether you're part of a traditional marriage, a same-sex partnership, a single mother-to-be, a new stepmother, an adoptive mom, or a mother in any other circumstance, you share in the joys and dilemmas that all mothers face. For the sake of practicality, we used traditional language throughout the book (by referring to fathers and husbands, for instance), but hope that you will feel included in the ideas even if the limitations of language and space inhibit us from using the exact terms that fit your situation.
>
> **All babies are welcome!** You may be giving birth to twins, triplets, or multiples; you may be adopting; your babies may have conditions we don't address; or you may have other children already in your family. We chose language reflecting common circumstances and invite you to apply the information to suit your life and your family.
>
> **Husbands and partners are welcome, too!** Throughout the book we talk directly to you and walk you through the process as if you are going through it alone, because *you* are the one becoming a mother! However, we encourage you to collaborate with your husband or partner whenever possible.

Being Your Best

As a mother-to-be, you are starting a lifelong adventure. So much potential lies ahead—so much hope and possibility! When you are expecting a baby and getting ready for the changes that will bring, you are truly at a new beginning.

As you embark on this journey, you will be embracing a new way of life. You will be bringing a precious soul into your family and expanding your relationships. Seeing through your baby's eyes, you will experience the world around you as if for the first time.

It's true that motherhood can change you. Your heart will grow. Your relationships will deepen. You will see people differently, as your husband or partner becomes a father, your parents become grandparents, and your friends and relatives become role models for your baby. Perhaps most significant of all, you will redefine yourself. You will forever identify as a mother—the central, unifying figure for a little person who depends on you. So yes, your life is going to change.

At the same time, you can also protect the amazing qualities that make you who you are. Your strengths and talents. Your sense of humor. Your style. The life lessons you've learned, the contributions you've made, your accomplishments, your principles, and your sense of self. You can choose a life in which you maintain and enhance the best of yourself, for you *and* your baby. By becoming a mother without losing yourself, you will welcome your baby in a way that honors all of who you are.

> *"I am reminded how powerful I can be not only as a mother, but a wife, friend, and professional. When I choose to do the things that will benefit me, they will ultimately benefit my family. It takes a lot of courage to start making decisions that you want, and it is amazing how people come to respect you for doing that."*
> —LENA, 6 MONTHS PREGNANT

Our Stories

As personal coaches, we work with women across the country to help each one create the life she wants. We've learned that every new mother has her own hopes and dreams, challenges to overcome, and distinctive ways of designing her life. As do we. We too used this process to become mothers without losing ourselves. Here are our stories.

Joelle. As a busy consultant, I found myself working evenings and weekends, feeling generally rushed and stressed out about life. Before I was even ready to be a mother, I could see this was no life for a baby. I wanted to be attentive, fun-loving, and relaxed as a mother—not harried and absent. I could see something seriously needed to change.

I started asking myself questions, re-envisioning my life, getting clear on my priorities, and making decisions that would make that kind of motherhood possible without compromising the career I was working so hard to achieve. Little by little, I started making room for a baby.

At work, I remodeled my business so that I could work a little less and make a little more. I kept the projects I loved and gave away the rest. I cut out the "extras" in my life—volunteering for a girls' club, being the recorder for my professional association, and doing small projects for an old client. At home, Tim and I sat down and sketched out our new lives. We figured out a way to take care of a baby while still making time for the things we loved to do on our own, like golfing, skiing, and reading. We found the daycare. We bought the SUV. It may sound crazy, but I literally had a color-coded calendar system that proved we could make it all work. When my maternity leave started—two weeks before Jackson was born—I was ready.

Having my first baby still wasn't easy. There were tears and late nights. There was stress and confusion. But I felt better able to handle it. I remember one night holding Jackson as he cried and cried. I felt tired, fat, and messy. And yet, I felt strangely . . . okay. I might have been clueless, but I wasn't out of control. Instead of falling apart as I'd once feared I might, I remember reassuring my son, "Don't worry. We'll figure this out." And somehow that's what we did.

Amy. When I became pregnant, I was nervous and excited. I knew that as a life coach who helps clients create balanced and fulfilled lives as mothers, I had better practice what I preach!

As I started down the path to motherhood, I thought about how much self-growth work I had done over the years. Despite all that effort, pregnancy was already challenging me in new ways. Many of my old, familiar issues started popping back up, like defining my worth by how much I get done and needing to do everything well.

At the same time, I was really excited about the baby! Married at 38, pregnant at 39, with a bonus gift of three stepdaughters and a career that I loved, I had almost everything I always dreamed about. I felt like I was holding my breath—afraid that I couldn't have it all, that I would be forced to give something up. "Can I really have all of this?" I kept wondering. "Is there going to be some catch?"

I dedicated myself to preserving the parts of my life I wanted to keep, planning for the baby I was so grateful to be having, and deciding what I didn't mind letting go. I carved out the four-month maternity leave I craved, put my convertible up for sale, and bought the crib we really wanted. I told my stepdaughters that I hoped they would see the baby as their brother not as their stepmother's child. I asked Mike for extra "Daddy duty" so I could pursue publishing this book and told friends I didn't want stuffed animals or blankets but did want prepared meals and chocolate chip cookies.

I posted the commitments I made to myself—my values, my beliefs, and my intention—on the wall next to my rocking chair. Months later, with Matt in my arms, I would read the words as I rocked him to sleep. Those words are still an anchor for me, keeping me tethered to my commitment to bring all of who I am to my son.

What You Might Experience

We can't tell you exactly what your life will look like, but we can tell you what you might experience when you take the steps to design your new life as a mother.

1. **You will feel ready** *to handle the big challenges of the first year.* When your baby arrives, you are better able to relax and enjoy the experience, having prepared emotionally *and* logistically.

2. **You will feel more confident** *and less guilty, tense, and overwhelmed as a new mother.* With the barrage of conflicting dos and don'ts for everything from feeding to sleeping to whether to go back to work, having a baby can seem overwhelming. Having a stronger sense of self helps you make the decisions that are right for *you.*

3. **You will be able to maintain a balance** *between your career, your baby, your partner and you.* When the challenges of new motherhood surface, you can minimize frustration and confusion by connecting back to everything you learned about who you are and what you believe.

4. **You will find solutions** *to help a new baby fit into your already busy life.* When there's too much to do and too little time to do it—a common complaint of new mothers—you can ask yourself what will best fit your intention for your family and do *that.* Everything else can wait.

5. **You will gain certainty** *that you are preparing to be the best mother you can be.*

In addition, your children will learn the importance you place on building a life of fulfillment and you will learn ways to ensure that you will be the kind of mother you most want to be.

A Life of Fulfillment

As a time of great excitement and change, the transition into new motherhood is the perfect opportunity to design your life. Take advantage! Embrace it!

By going through this process, you prepare for motherhood in a powerful way. This is not about creating your baby's life, it's about creating a life into which you want to bring a baby. Being your best, most complete, fulfilled self will support you, your baby, and your family.

When the time comes, you will give birth to your baby and also your new life. You will thrive—not just survive—the first year of motherhood. The transition into motherhood only happens once. Make it amazing.

OUR PHILOSOPHY

In helping you clarify what is important to you, it only seems fair that we share what's important to us. We based this process on our own core values and beliefs. Some of these ideas may resonate with you immediately. Some may challenge you, and others may expand your thinking. We invite you to weigh our beliefs against your own as a way to begin the process of becoming more fully *you* in preparation for motherhood.

✓ *Life is going to change. How you respond is up to you.* If you're pregnant now, you've probably already been warned that life is going to change—sometimes in less-than-encouraging ways. "You just wait," your friends smirk, implying that you will never again have a relaxing bath, a pedicure, or a romantic evening. "You'd better enjoy it now," they caution as you head off for a vacation, as if you'll never leave your house again once the baby arrives. They are your friends, you love them, and you know they mean well. "Your life is going to be different," they tell you, and you probably already know this to be true. We want you to see that you have some choice in *how* your life will be different, and a lot of choice in how you'll respond. This book is about choosing who you want to be as a mother and how much easier and enjoyable new motherhood is when you take charge.

✓ *You can have it all, as long as you know what your "all" is.* This book is about creating your ideal life. We want you to know that this isn't an empty promise to "have it all." In fact, you may have to make some sacrifices to get what you want. It *is* a promise to help you figure out what's most important to you, based on your values and priorities. When a new baby comes into your life, the way you express those values and priorities may change, but what's important to you will fundamentally be the same. When you prioritize based on what's important to you, you may not "have it all" in the sense of having money, fame, a great figure, the gorgeous husband, and every possible luxury. However, you *feel* like you have it all because you have everything that's important to *you*.

✓ *You can be fulfilled both inside and outside your role as a mother.* When you become a mother, you do not cease being you. Becoming a mother enriches your identity; it doesn't replace it. Until now, you have found fulfillment in a variety of relationships, endeavors, and experiences *all without having a baby*. Now, you will also find fulfillment in motherhood. You do not have to choose between yourself and your baby. You can be who you are already while adding new dimensions. What an abundant gift!

✓ *We live in an abundant world.* We believe in open minds, creativity, and positive thinking. Some people dwell in the impossible. They refuse to consider options, and they get stuck believing that what they want can't happen. We find this kind of thinking limiting. We see enormous power in believing that there *is* a way to your goals, through your obstacles, and into the life you want to create.

✓ *When you take care of yourself, you are a better mother.* Babies thrive in environments that are secure, stable, and loving. You will be best able to provide that when *you* feel secure, stable, and loving. We believe you will be less frustrated, more patient, more present, and a better role model for your children when you feel fulfilled. Fulfillment that comes from living a life that reflects who you really are. Taking the time to create that life is as important as painting the room, folding tiny clothes, and learning to sing nursery rhymes. We believe it's even more so.

USING THIS BOOK

When to Read It

Each woman has her own approach to reading *Becoming a Mother*. Some women jump in and read the book in their first trimester, eager to contemplate their new life with a baby. Others wait until the last minute, busy with preparation for labor and delivery or activities in their current life. Any time you choose to read this book is the right time, even if you are *not* expecting a baby. The ideas are just as valuable if you are thinking about becoming a mother or wanting to make life changes after your baby has arrived.

What's Inside

Each chapter guides you through a step-by-step process with an explanation of the topic, what you will be doing, why it is important, and what other women have experienced and learned. There is also a section called **Finding Your Own Way** in each chapter with something simple and concrete to do or think about right away. Additional exercises, examples, and blank worksheets are available at the end of each chapter in a section called **A Closer Look**.

Throughout the book, we offer a series of techniques to help you make the most of your process. These **Lessons in Becoming a Mother** include topics like "Wondering, Not Worrying" and "Asking for What You Want." Each lesson will serve you now, after the baby arrives, and throughout your life.

At the back of the book, we include an area called **Keepsakes** with blank worksheets to record your most memorable ideas. Use the worksheets as a guide, but capture what is important to *you*. We encourage you to create notes that you can keep in a journal, place in a binder, or put up on a wall—enabling you to refer back to your learning often throughout your first year as a mother.

Don't miss the sections called **Mother's Helper** and our **Top Ten Tips** at the end of the book where we share secrets on how to make the first year easier from our work with other empowered mothers. Finally, **We're Here to Help You!** describes the wealth of electronic worksheets, tools, and stories on our website to support you in *Becoming a Mother*. You can find these at **www.empoweredmotherhood.com**.

What to Do

There are many ways to move through the process. You are welcome to just read the book and skip the exercises, skimming through and taking what you need. You can try doing the exercises in your head, using the examples and anecdotes to spark ideas for your life. Or take your time, journaling your thoughts and diligently working with every exercise and extra resource offered. Different women spend as little as a few days or several months in the book. You're in a busy time with much to think about and do; you can come in and out of your process as necessary. Find your own way of learning and doing this process.

What You Will Need

You will need a sincere effort, the willingness to make honest decisions, a belief that you can create what you want, and a commitment to yourself, your baby, and your family. Other than that, you will need a pen or pencil and some paper. Many women choose to buy a special journal to use with the book while others scribble notes in the margins and worksheets.

What to Remember

The ideas contained in this book are intended to help you explore your thoughts, clarify what's important to you, and go after what you want for your new life. Of course, the way you want life to be isn't always the way it is. Life might turn the plans you make in this book upside down. Your body may heal more quickly than you imagined, your husband or partner might change jobs, or your baby might have its own agenda! You also may choose to change your own plans. Perhaps you decide to stay on maternity leave a little longer—maybe a month, maybe a year, maybe forever. Or you might decide to go racing back to work sooner than expected. You may not even *want* to plan your whole life. The surprises babies bring are half the fun! We encourage you to plan as much or as little as you like. Either way, when you're clear about who you are and what's important to you, you're better equipped to handle everything life throws your way.

LESSONS IN
BECOMING A MOTHER

At the end of every chapter is a special lesson to help you make the most of your process of *Becoming a Mother*. Here is a sneak preview!

Lesson 1: Wondering, not Worrying

Turn your concerns into curiosity and possibilities.

Lesson 2: Mother's Intuition

Listen to your truth.

Lesson 3: Values-Centered Living

Use your values to guide your daily actions and decisions.

Lesson 4: Handling Judgment

Stand confident in the face of judgment.

Lesson 5: Remembering What's Most Important

Honor your true priorities.

Lesson 6: Saying No

Say no gracefully with certainty and confidence.

Lesson 7: Fighting Fear

Handle the fears that can accompany new motherhood.

Lesson 8: The Gift of Gratitude

Find joy in any circumstance.

Lesson 9: Asking for What You Want

Boldly make requests and get what you need.

Lesson 10: Savoring Every Moment

Be present and relish every moment.

CHAPTER ONE

Step 1
EXPLORING NEW MOTHERHOOD

"Your vision will become clear only when you look into your heart.
Who looks outside, dreams. Who looks inside, awakens."
—*Carl Jung*

Motherhood is full of firsts. The first signs of pregnancy. The first time you feel the baby move. The first contraction. The first time you see your baby's face. At that moment you experience one more first—the first time you become somebody's mother.

To prepare for that moment and the transformation of your life that will follow, we invite you to explore what motherhood is *for you*. Whether you're a first-time expectant mother or have had a baby before, you've never been *here*—expecting this child at this time of your life with these kinds of experiences behind you. No matter how accomplished you are in any of the areas of your life, you're still brand new at *this*. Scary? A little—especially for those who are used to having it all figured out. But it's also incredibly thrilling, for who knows what may lie ahead?

When you experience something for the first time, you simply don't know what to expect. Your senses are heightened. Your antennae are up. You are more open to possibilities and less likely to jump to conclusions. Exploration is about learning. You get to ask as many questions as you want. You have permission to do things shakily and be forgiven for not being perfect. Now, before your baby is born, you have nothing to lose. This is your chance to discover.

As you prepare to become a mother, you may be filled with apprehension, anticipation, and excitement. In this chapter, you take your first steps. You're about to explore new motherhood.

Asking Questions, Finding Answers

Who do you want to be as a mother? Who do you *not* want to be? What images are you holding onto, and how do they limit or expand your possibilities? In this chapter, you will explore the domain of new motherhood. In your exploration, you will ask yourself key questions and take time to hear your own answers.

We get you started with a series of questions later in this chapter and encourage you to ask your own. You will consider questions about who you are becoming, how your life will change, and what you've gotten yourself into. Essentially, your exploration is about investigating your views on motherhood, your strengths, your needs, your fears, and your hopes as you enter your first year as a mother. Listening to your thoughts will eventually lead to reassurance, courage, and empowerment as you design the life you want.

> *"No one ever asks you about you! They tell you about labor and delivery and give you all kinds of advice, but you don't get to think about what you really want for yourself. It was gratifying to find out that I do have so many answers of my own!"*   —DEBRA, 7 MONTHS PREGNANT

An important part of this process is looking inward. It's much more common for women to look *outward* for advice and answers to their questions about impending motherhood than to look for the answers inside themselves. This is the time to awaken to all of *your* feelings about having a baby. You can allow yourself to be scared, surprised, embarrassed, stumped, or delighted by what you find. And whatever you discover is just perfect.

> *"I really wanted to bring my husband into this process, so I asked him questions from his perspective. Of course, he kept making jokes like answering 'diapers' when I asked what scares him the most about becoming a father. But, there was a lot of sweetness too. When I asked him what he most wanted to share with the baby, he said 'Everything.'"*   —ERICA, 8 MONTHS PREGNANT

Clearing Your Mind

Exploring opens and clears your mind—an important step to becoming a mother, when you're learning something so new. As a mother, you will often be called upon to be all-knowing. Your kids will turn to you with confidence and adoration, secure in the knowledge that you know how to painlessly remove a splinter, tie the perfect bow, and obliterate monsters.

But not now. Not today. Today you get to ask the questions. You get to *not* know, and that not knowing allows you to open your mind.

As a result of your exploration, you'll be able to identify:

- The barriers
- The solutions
- The resources
- The misconceptions
- The emotions
- The possibilities

that lie ahead on the path to new motherhood.

The goal is to clear away the clutter in your mind—the clutter caused by fears, hopes, expectations, opinions, and judgments that seem to pile up on every new mother. It's like cleaning out a closet: Sometimes you can't get it all organized until you take everything out and really see what you are dealing with. Then you can determine what's most valuable and what's simply getting in the way. As you ask and answer questions throughout this chapter, be prepared to keep the most meaningful ideas and throw out the rest as one way of opening up to your new life.

EXPECTANT MOTHERS CLEAR THEIR MINDS!

"I'm getting a little nervous about having the baby! It seems like it's coming so quickly, and I don't have anything ready! I'm just a little freaked out about how quickly it's snuck up on me." —ROSA

"I've always been career-oriented, really goal-oriented. I can't remember a time in my life when I wasn't planning for what I was going to do. With me it's always been, 'What's next? What more can I do? What else can I achieve?' I really enjoyed all of that for many, many years. Now just being part of my family and being a part of the community is starting to take on a more important level in my life." —WENDY

"I am so excited to meet the little guy! It's been an amazing experience to feel him moving all the time and see the ultrasounds and all of that. I'm really excited to meet him and see what he's like."   —JULIA

"All of my experiences in life will help me deal with having a new baby. I'm going to try to bring all my knowledge and all my skills to it. With a baby, you can't do a do-over!"   —PAULA

"How am I going to do this? How am I going to balance professional and personal life in a way that I feel like I am doing well on both sides? How do I work with my husband, who is also a professional, and trying to balance out our joint responsibility of being parents as well as our aspirations in our own separate professions?"   —HEATHER

"Getting married three years ago was a really big deal, and it's been a great relationship, and this is like the next layer. It occupies my thoughts! I can't wait to meet this child!"   —HOLLY

"I'm very proud of how hard I've worked and how successful I have managed to be. There have been parts of my journey that were not so wonderful, but I've kept my eye on the prize, and moving in that direction, and it finally happened! Now I have to figure out what it all looks like with a baby."   —RACHEL

"What if I'm not good with a baby? What would I do?"   —SYDNEY

"I think the best thing we can do as women is to support ourselves in all the different choices that we make. It's about all the different options that we have and really opening our mind to what those options are."   —MEGGIN

FINDING YOUR OWN WAY
Exploring Your Thoughts

Now you will explore your hopes and fears about your new life as a mother. Below, we've given you several questions designed to jumpstart your thinking. At the end of the chapter in the section we call "A Closer Look," you'll find additional questions for your exploration. Spend some time with these questions. You may just want to turn them over in your mind, you may want to write about them in a journal, or you may want to take some notes right here in this book. In the "Keepsakes" section at the back of the book, we have included a special page ("My Exploration") for you to record your ideas.

Before you begin, get in the exploring frame of mind. A good explorer has a great attitude—one that is wide open and curious. Exploring with a narrow mind shuts out the unexpected and spontaneous. If you are too certain of what you will find, you might miss the real treasure. When you explore without assumptions or expectations, your heart has a chance to lead the way.

Take a moment right now and ask yourself the following questions. Don't over think, just go with your immediate thoughts.

- ❷ What excites me about motherhood?
- ❷ What parts of myself am I afraid of losing?
- ❷ What do I want to share with my baby?
- ❷ What would help me the most in the first year?
- ❷ What do I need to let go of before the baby is born?

Look over your answers. What do you notice? Are your answers positive? Negative? Was it easy to come up with some thoughts or do you need more time to ponder? How did it feel to do a little exploring? One mom-to-be, Mimi, was pleasantly surprised, "As I did my exploration, I discovered more about myself than I expected. I realized that I had been thinking a lot about other people's expectations, but had not thought very much about my own."

Have fun exploring! Enjoy delving into the questions and the opportunity to say what you feel, if only to yourself. In this process you have the chance to speak from your heart, like Allie, "I'm looking forward to loving and nurturing another individual who is pure and open," and Camille, "What excites me about motherhood? This is not something I can put in words except that I get excited when I feel it moving around in there." You can speak your truth like Mary, "I'm scared that I won't have the necessary patience," or Chandra, "I don't want my parenting to be a string of tasks." Nothing you say can be wrong when you're discovering what you feel.

Now, continue your exploration using the questions in "A Closer Look" as well as your own. This is a perfect time to invite your husband or partner to participate, as these questions always spark interesting conversations. Tease out your thoughts with a friend, a coach, or fellow expecting mother. Turn over the questions at different times of the day and various locations—see what you think during the commute to work, how your answers flow while taking a bubble bath, or what insights emerge as you walk through the park. There is no right way to explore. Relax, be open, and see what there is to see.

KEEPSAKE

Write down your most intriguing thoughts in the "My Exploration" worksheet in the "Keepsakes" section in Appendix A or use your own journal or notebook.

TIPS FOR EXPLORING _____

- Slow down and give yourself permission to ponder.
- Be a new mother, even if you've been down this road before.
- Drop any old assumptions and start fresh.
- Be fascinated, not judgmental, of your answers.
- Allow yourself to wonder, not worry.
- Be ruthlessly honest.
- Avoid thinking too hard, searching for the "right" answer, or worrying about what it all means.

"At first I didn't want to take the time to write down all the answers, I thought I could just answer them in my head. But, as I started to write—more came out than I thought. It's so important to give yourself room to explore."
—KYLA, 8 MONTHS PREGNANT

Common Experiences _____

Discovery can be scary. It takes you into unknown territory. Trekking into your thoughts may lead to pleasant and unpleasant surprises. Some women even come across ideas they don't want to face. They also encounter hidden strengths and power. Be open to whatever turns up.

Many expecting mothers have found great learning in their inner investigations. Here are some common issues that surface in the discovery stage.

Making Connections. Exploring ideas about motherhood often results in an assorted collection of ideas. As they review their thoughts, many women find themselves connecting these ideas in interesting and unexpected ways.

Beth was a mother-to-be who discovered in her exploration that:

- At 40, she was nervous about being an "older mother."
- She loved a clean house and an orderly life.
- She was afraid she would lose that sense of order.
- She wanted time for herself.
- She expected her baby could help her "loosen up."
- She hoped her baby would help her take risks and discover new parts of herself.

These seemingly disparate ideas came together for Beth as she thought about them all at once.

For instance, she saw that her forty years of life experience gave her an advantage. She knew how to run a household and manage a complex life. Instead of worrying about her age, she saw how it could help her preserve the kind of home and lifestyle she loved. Another idea also dawned on her. Perhaps the newness of a baby would challenge her to discover a way of life that was less orderly and more playful and fun. This allowed her to not worry so much about getting time for herself and become eager to spend time with her baby.

The ideas that surface in exploration often mingle in interesting, unusual ways—ways that can start you thinking creatively about becoming a mother.

Finding Fear. Many women harbor some share of terror at the prospect of becoming a new mother! Here are a just few common fears expectant mothers have found lurking in their exploration.

- Fear of their bodies changing, for the worse.
- Fear of not being up to the challenge.
- Fear that they will have to give up the careers they worked so hard for.
- Fear that they won't be able to quit their job if they really want to.
- Fear about money and what everything will cost.
- Fear about the relationship with their husbands or partners changing.
- Fear about not being able to diaper/feed/hold/soothe/dress/raise a baby.

The discovery process can highlight these fears as it starts to sink in even more that you are, in fact, having a baby, and your life is going to change—soon. It's normal and natural to have these fears. Later, we will discuss productive ways to tackle them. For now, just notice them and see what there is to learn.

Recognizing Opportunities for Change. The discovery process requires looking in the mirror. Sometimes the image looking back is less than flattering. Somewhat sheepishly, Kyla confessed that her vision of motherhood was "Pretty selfish! I realized that part of what I was looking forward to was the spotlight of being a mother—that I would be special and important and that this baby would be all mine!" Even though the idea made her smile (what a joy it would be to be so central in someone's life!), it also made Kyla uncomfortable. It seemed to her a self-centered way of thinking about motherhood. She started looking for ways she could revel in her new role as a mother while at the same time considering her baby. As she reflected, she found, "I want to learn to love selflessly and to break my heart wide open." Even though Kyla was challenged by what she found in her exploration, it also presented new possibilities.

Uncovering Surprising Emotions. Exploring ideas about motherhood can be an emotional endeavor. "I didn't expect that asking myself these questions would stir things up," Daphne reported. "When I thought about who I most wanted to be a part of my life in the first year of motherhood, I was hit with a wave of sadness. I started thinking of all the people who have died—my father, my grandmother—and how hard it is that they won't see my child." Daphne had not known that grief was there until she looked closely into her emotions about becoming a new mother. By becoming conscious and acknowledging those feelings, Daphne was able to honor the people she loved and missed even though they could no longer be with her. Her discovery revealed an aspect of motherhood she didn't even know was there.

Developing a Stronger Sense of Self. Many women come away from their exploration stronger in their identities. Almost every new mother we coach completes her discovery with new insight as to what she wants for her baby.

"I want my child to know that she is inherently worthwhile," said Liz.

"Peace of heart. A feeling of belonging and security. Knowing that he is loved, seen, and respected. That is what I want to share with our baby," reflected Emily.

"I want to share that kind of love that only parents and children share and to learn how to raise twins to be decent, respectful, joyous little people," added Simone.

You may discover fear and questions in your exploration, but you may also discover the heart of a mother. By searching inside for your thoughts about motherhood, you may start to find your special way of mothering—which will one day be your gift to your baby.

Discovering Yourself as a Mother

Becoming a mother is about discovering yourself.

As you explored motherhood in this chapter, you asked questions and listened to your answers. Perhaps you have made some new discoveries about how you feel, what you think, what you expect, and what might challenge you in your new life. You've begun to find your own truths, both positive and negative. You may have come up against some strong opinions. You may also have identified fears or beliefs that are limiting you and even found some questions you aren't quite ready to answer. The process is all about taking your first steps, walking around this place in your life, and getting your footing for the journey into new motherhood.

By looking honestly into your heart, you have started the mental, emotional, and intellectual preparation that complements the physical preparation of pregnancy. You have made an enormous investment in yourself and your new baby—one that will pay you back dividends as you become a mother with a clearer sense of yourself.

 An Inquiry for You   What can I discover?

C O N G R A T U L A T I O N S !

You have just completed your first step – your exploration! We want to acknowledge you for

- Valuing what you think.
- Taking time to listen to yourself.
- Being open and curious.
- Welcoming both the positive and the negative.
- Connecting from the heart with what motherhood is about *for* you.

A Closer Look

Exercise: Furthering Your Exploration

You have already begun your exploration into motherhood by asking yourself some powerful questions. Here, we offer more questions to expand your thinking about your new life. *Be sure to capture your thoughts in "My Exploration" in the "Keepsakes" section in Appendix A.*

- ❷ What really scares me about becoming a mother?
- ❷ What could be my biggest strengths as a mother? My biggest challenges?
- ❷ What do I love about my life now that I don't want to give up after the baby is born?
- ❷ What in my life could I give up? What *do* I want to change?
- ❷ What do I want to learn from being a mother?
- ❷ What people do I want to include as part of our life in that first year?
- ❷ What parts of my parents' parenting style would I like to keep?
- ❷ What am I afraid of passing onto my child from my own childhood?
- ❷ How do I expect my relationships to change after the baby is born? With my husband or partner, family, friends, colleagues?
- ❷ What has already changed just by being pregnant?
- ❷ What do I think my child wants for me?
- ❷ As a mother, I should…
- ❷ I hope I…
- ❷ I hope I don't…
- ❷ I wonder…
- ❷ I expect…
- ❷ What else do I want to ask myself?

EXTRA RESOURCES

An electronic version of the questions is available at **www.empoweredmotherhood.com,** as well as other women's thoughts on approaching motherhood and a chance to share your own.

Lessons in BECOMING A MOTHER

Lesson 1 **Wondering, Not Worrying**

Turn your concerns into curiosity and possibilities.

"How can I be somebody's mother? I can barely keep my own act together!"
"What if the epidural doesn't work?"
"What if I don't like being a mother? There's no going back!"
"What was that kick? Was that normal? Is the baby all right?"

There's no doubt—having a baby can stir up a lot of worries. Those little voices in your head go crazy when they sense a big change coming. "You should be careful!" they holler. "Do you really know what you are doing?" Whether you're worrying about weight gain or hassling over hospitals, there are dozens of ways to work yourself up.

Worrying about the future is normal but not helpful. It may make you feel as if you're doing something about your concerns because you're thinking about them all the time. But worrying gets you nowhere. It simply leads you around in circles, landing you right back where you started, chewing on the same old fears and anxieties. You need a way out of this cycle.

Instead of worrying, turn to wonder.

Unlike worry, wonder draws you forward. When you wonder, you get curious and explore new ideas and possibilities. Wonder raises fresh thoughts, helping you let go of fears and find solutions to problems. It leads you into the future with an open, trusting mind.

You can transform worry into wonder with just a twist of your thinking. Below are some examples of how moms-to-be have turned their worries into wonder. Notice how different the second statement feels from the first.

Grace's Worry: What if people respect me less as a professional after I have a baby?
Grace's Wonder: I wonder what it will feel like to be a mother who is also a professional.

Lucia's Worry: What if we can't afford to live the life I have in mind?
Lucia's Wonder: I wonder how our priorities and values will shift with a new baby and a new life.

Margot's Worry: What if I lose touch with my friends?
Margot's Wonder: I wonder what new ways my friends and I will find to relate to each other.

Angela's Worry: What if nobody can care for my baby like I can? What if daycare isn't as good as I hope?
Angela's Wonder: I wonder who will emerge as the right caregiver for my baby when I'm not there. I wonder what he or she will be like.

Shelly's Worry: How am I going to fit all of this into my life?
Shelly's Wonder: I wonder how my life will look.

In each of these examples the expecting mothers were anticipating their babies by worrying, blocking any kind of creative thought. By shifting their thinking to wonder, they were able to let go of the stress and start imagining the possibilities. Instead of spending their time on the "what ifs" of new motherhood, these women were able to enjoy the magic and beauty of new life.

We want the same for you. In the coming months, pay close attention to what's worrying you. Then turn to wonder instead and see how it suddenly changes your view for the better.

CHAPTER TWO

Step 2
IMAGINING YOUR IDEAL FIRST YEAR

"Without leaps of imagination, or dreaming, we lose the excitement of possibilities. Dreaming, after all, is a form of planning."
—*Gloria Steinem*

Since you found out you were having a baby, you have dreamed of her arrival. Maybe you've pictured her rosy cheeks, her velvet skin, her powdery scent. Along with dreams about your new baby, it's time to start dreaming about the new life you will live as a mother. You do this by using your imagination.

Living life from imagination makes anything possible. Imagination knows no limits. It doesn't say, "I can't" or "I'll never" or "that won't ever happen for me." Instead, imagination wonders and wishes.

In the last chapter you explored some of your hopes and fears about becoming a mother. In doing that exploration, you thought about what *is*, what you think and feel right now. In this chapter, you imagine what you will think and feel in the future—you will dream about what *if*.

Here, you let loose your imagination and envision your ideal first year. This is your chance to daydream, to make your wish, to create a picture of what your new life as a mother *could* be if anything were possible. Trust us, there will be plenty of time for reality later. Just take a moment now to enter the life of your dreams.

Living Life from Imagination

Michelangelo said, "Refuse to allow yourself to have low expectations about what you're capable of creating. The greater danger is not that your hopes are too high and you fail to reach them; it's that they're too low and you do." In this chapter we invite you to proclaim your highest hopes for motherhood.

The goal is to imagine your ideal first year as a mother. What would a perfect year look like? What if you *could* have it all? Go ahead, live a little! Find out what "ideal" really means for you.

For example, imagine a day with your baby. Would "perfect" be strolling along sexy and sassy with your baby at your side, shopping in the latest boutiques? Or would it be lounging in pajamas all day long with nothing to do but be mama? Would "ideal" mean being the can-do businesswoman with a happy family? Would it mean a little time for yourself? A trip to the spa? A good jog? Time with your hobby? Time with your hubby? A playgroup full of other brand new mothers, every one of them as clueless and hopeful as you?

As you'll see, the process of imagining can take many forms, from creating a wish list to dreaming a little about the future. We call the result your *vision*. Your vision gives you a way of looking into the future, even when you're not sure what the future holds. It's also an effective way to find clarity about the life you want to create. The idea is to take a time out from reality and live life from imagination.

Using Your Intuition

Unlike daydreaming, imagining your future isn't just an escape (although there's something to be said for that, too). Even if you've been dreaming about life with a baby for years, imagining your first year is not about simply revisiting those ideas. It involves actively engaging with ideal images that reflect who you really want to be, how you want to live, and what your life will be like.

This kind of dreaming taps into your intuition, bringing you new awareness about motherhood as you will experience it. Using your imagination this way lets your mind and heart tell you things you may have not even realized. A wealth of information awaits when you let your inner voice speak.

When you imagine your future, you shut off the practical side of your brain— the side that plans and worries and wants to be realistic. You give your intuition free rein. You let wisdom and truth whisper their insights without being drowned out by the clamor of everyday life. Later, you will attend to practicalities. But now, in your imagination, you get to simply tune them out.

> *"It was nice being able to think about what my life could be without getting hung up on how to get there. I like how I felt afterwards. It put a picture in my head that I can meditate on and bring to my baby."*   —NINA, 6 MONTHS PREGNANT

Dreaming is to thinking like playing is to working. They are both important. They balance each other. But in a busy life, many women seldom take time to just play with their ideas. Instead of admiring happy thoughts in their purest state, they drop them before they even blossom. They squelch them with questions of how those ideas could ever happen or reasons why they won't. In your imagination, you can freely discover the beauty and potential in your biggest thoughts, your wildest dreams, and your highest aspirations. Those dreams then fill a very practical purpose—they give you a clearer idea of what you want for this new life and the ability to start to create it.

> *"I'm the type of person who powers through everything. It was hard, at first, to stop and just listen to myself. But I had some pretty amazing things pop up on my wish list, like a six-month maternity leave that I would have otherwise have judged as impractical. Maybe I should let myself dream a little more often."*
> —DANIELA, 8 MONTHS PREGNANT

The Meaning of Dreaming

The life you dream of may not be the one you create. You might learn new things about yourself later in this process that change your mind about what you really want. And let's face it: Your baby will have his or her *own* ideas about what life should be like! So don't worry about if you imagine a life that's not possible. Allow yourself to be open. This is not about envisioning your exact future. It's about freeing your mind, having some fun, being creative, and seeing what there is to learn.

The whole process boils down to three easy steps:

1. Tap into your imagination.
2. Notice what's there.
3. Ask what it means to you.

Then use that learning to inform you as you move closer to designing your new life as a mother.

For instance, let's say that your vision of the ideal first year has you hiking up a mountain with your baby in a backpack. You might not like to hike. But this scene has something to offer about what might be important to you: exercise, fresh air, family time with your baby—maybe even a vacation. Regardless of whether you ever go hiking in your first year as a mother, you have nevertheless uncovered something significant—a list of things that you want to maintain in your life after you've had your baby.

Notice that this process isn't just about dreaming. It's also about discovering meaning. You are learning about yourself and what might be important when your real baby actually arrives.

Here are some more examples.

Let's say you imagine new people around you with their babies. What might it mean? You may be craving camaraderie and companionship. Or maybe you're concerned about being alone in your new role. Perhaps you make a wish list that includes lots of snuggle time with your baby. What might that tell you? Could it mean that you want to slow down your schedule or take an extra-long maternity leave (maybe forever)? Or maybe your ideal first year includes a weekly date night with your husband or partner. What might that say to you? It could mean that you want to maintain connection so your husband or partner doesn't feel replaced by the baby, that you want to be sure to get out of the house, or that you want to add structure to your life by scheduling some regular couple time.

Remember as you let your imagination take flight that there is no right way to interpret your thoughts. You can interpret them in limitless ways. Keep asking what the ideas and images you imagine mean *to you*.

> *"My vision really made me think. I saw myself sitting alone at a café on a sunny day catching up on some work. My baby wasn't with me, but I could tell that he was somewhere safe and loving. I felt free and calm. I realized that I want great childcare—a way to continue with my career goals without feeling like a horrible mother. And seeing the café instead of my office, maybe I need to think about work from a different angle!"*   —GINNY, 6 MONTHS PREGNANT

FINDING YOUR OWN WAY
Creating Your Vision

Now is your chance to play! You are about to create a vision of your ideal first year as a mother. Below, we give you a taste of our favorite ways to create a vision, along with some other suggestions that might appeal to you. At the end of the chapter in "A Closer Look," we provide more detailed exercises that you can use to expand and complete your vision. You can build your vision with your husband or partner or share what you each created on your own. Whether you finish with a complete picture or just a few glimpses of your life ahead, take pleasure in the process!

Visualizing. One approach is to visualize your ideal first year. Really *see* it. Let pictures of your future life as a mother play in your mind, like a movie or a slide show. Close your eyes, relax, and take a few minutes to imagine one ideal scene from your first year as a mother. Let your intuition run the show. Try it now.

What popped into your head? Where were you? Who was there? What were you doing? What meaning do you see in your dreaming? Take notes to capture your initial vision as well as any thoughts and feelings it generated.

Making a Wish. Another way to tap into your creativity is to create a giant wish list of everything you desire for your first year of motherhood. We love to do this on the floor using big empty sheets of paper and colored pens and pencils, but you can brainstorm on the computer, on a sketchpad, in your PDA, on decorative stationery, or in your head.

Make a mini wish list right now. Grab a piece of paper and a pen and give yourself five minutes to create a wish list of things that you absolutely want for your first year as a mother. Think across your life from your new baby, to your husband or partner, to your career and passions, to family and friends!

What was that like for you? What do you notice about this preliminary wish list? How do your wishes combine to paint a picture of life as a mother?

Do Something Else! There are limitless other ways to imagine. Sketch your vision, paint it in vivid color on canvas, or handwrite a letter to your fairy godmother. We know one expectant mother who loves charts; she had a heyday brainstorming for her first year in a spreadsheet. Another covered a wall with ideas on sticky notes. Some women love to make collages. Every mom-to-be may do this differently, experimenting with ways to make her vision one of a kind.

Take time now to put down this book and spend some time envisioning your future. Continue imagining in any way you wish. In "A Closer Look," we provide a full script to guide you through an extended visualization of your new life, suggestions on adding to your wish list, and an exercise to create an easy collage representing your ideal first year.

KEEPSAKE

Write down the key elements from your imaginings in the "My Vision" worksheet in the "Keepsakes" section in Appendix A or in your own journal or notebook.

TIPS FOR FREEING YOUR IMAGINATION

- Stay in possibility. Keep saying the words, "If it were somehow possible, I would really like…"
- Suspend judgment. Banish doubts, what-ifs, or that looming question, "But how?"
- Be spontaneous. Let your right brain—the creative, intuitive side—take charge. Allow your mind to wander. The goal is to gain momentum in your thinking and not let any kind of rules slow you down.
- Welcome everything. No second-guessing yourself. There is no right or wrong, only learning.
- Set the tone. Play some music, light a few candles, or maybe break out the chocolate! Do whatever it takes to be comfortable and inspired. Clear everything else away and remove any distractions.

Common Experiences

Given the chance to roam freely, your imagination has so much to reveal. Below are some of the experiences other expecting mothers have found as they've gone through this process.

Having Trouble Getting Started. You may find it takes you a while to let loose. Janis noticed as she made a long wish list for a stellar first year of motherhood that she was putting down a lot of small stuff like buying a baby wipes warmer and organizing her CDs. But when she "hit the personal growth category," she said, "my list got more intense and out of the box. Deeper." The more time she spent with the list, the more she moved from the superficial to the sublime. Sometimes it takes take time, patience, and persistence to get to the point where the ideas really flow.

Getting Realistic Too Soon. Many women realize that being too realistic or too skeptical gets in the way of dreaming. Often your brain pulls you out of creativity and into practicality. Most women have to remind themselves to stay in "what if" and away from "but how?" You'll know you're really dreaming when your dreams take on a fairy-tale quality. (No one seems to visualize a crying, poopy baby!)

Envisioning the Unexpected. Your vision may startle you. This happened to Leticia. When daydreaming about her first year as a mother, suddenly her sister Rita showed up in the picture. Leticia and her sister had not been close for years, yet she saw a moving vision of Rita holding the baby. It made Leticia realize how profoundly she wanted her baby to know his aunt and inspired her to work on the relationship with her sister.

Anya was also surprised by what she saw for her first year. "I was really interested to see that my *job* was not on the wish list I made, nor was it in my collage. Hmmmm." As in so many places throughout the process of becoming a mother, surprises open the door to new learning.

Confirming Your Expectations. Sometimes, dreaming doesn't raise any surprises at all but rather confirms your view of motherhood the way you think it should be. Simone saw herself on a Disney cruise with her twin baby girls, her husband, and her dad. Everyone was happy and content on the balcony under the sun. Even as the picture made her laugh ("Can I go there now?"), she could see it held themes that were dear to her heart: family, freedom, and fun. Even when it doesn't expose anything new, visioning can reinforce what's important to you—a valuable reminder as life begins to change.

A Sense of Serenity—or Stress. Envisioning an ideal first year is often a crystallizing moment. Many women see for the first time a cohesive picture of their lives with a baby. Being shown an image of your future can be soothing or scary, depending on what you see.

One mother reported a sense of relief: After random thoughts of motherhood drifting through her mind for months, it felt good to collect her hopes and dreams in one place. Another felt a little overwhelmed and disappointed that her real life was so far from her vision.

Whether you feel reassured or rattled, the visioning process will often lead to clarity about what you do and don't want to create.

Your Ideal First Year

In your imagination, life can be perfect.

You now have a vision of your first year as a mother. Whether that vision is a series of images, a list, or just a general sense of what you'd love your life to be, it will serve as a guide to your future. You may not necessarily create the ideal life you've envisioned, but it's a beginning.

Your dreams about motherhood are the essence of the new life you're creating. By giving yourself permission to fantasize, you've freed yourself from the limits of reality and entered the realm of possibility.

As you move forward in *Becoming a Mother,* hold onto that optimistic idealism! In the coming chapters, you will come closer to living those sweet dreams.

 Where is my vision leading me?

C O N G R A T U L A T I O N S !

You have just completed your vision for your ideal first year as a mother. We want to acknowledge you for

- Giving yourself permission to dream.
- Listening to your intuition.
- Letting go of the "how."
- Thinking without limits.
- Living life from imagination.

A Closer Look

Below we give you three exercises to help you expand your vision of motherhood. You can choose to do one, two, or all three! Using different methods to access your imagination and listen to your intuition helps paint a full picture of your ideal first year.

EXTRA RESOURCES

A digital recording of us coaching you through visualizing your first year is available at **www.empoweredmotherhood.com**. You can just sit back, relax, and hit play!

Exercise 1: Visualizing Your First Year

This visualization includes a script you can use to imagine your first year as a mother. To get the most out of this exercise, you will want to put down the book and prepare for some quiet time and reflection.

- **Getting ready**. The most powerful way to visualize is to close your eyes and have someone guide you so your mind can wander freely. You may wish to have someone—a girlfriend, your husband or partner, a coach, or another mom-to-be—slowly read the script below aloud while you visualize. Ask him or her to be your scribe and take notes as you describe your vision. You may also read the script first and then go through the visualization unguided, from memory. Some mothers tape themselves reading the script and then play it back. You don't have to follow the script word for word. It is more important to allow the *spirit* of the exercise to open your mind, letting it wander freely.

  You will need a comfortable place to sit or lie down. Make sure there will be no distractions and that you will be undisturbed for about ten or fifteen minutes. Give yourself plenty of time during the visualization to see the picture your mind creates. Notice the details. Hear the words. Feel the emotions. Ready? Let's begin.

- **Visualizing.** Lie down, relax, and clear your mind. Close your eyes. Take a few deep breaths and release any tension. Let your mind become quiet. Continue this for a few moments until you feel completely relaxed, calm, and comfortable.

Imagine yourself in the future.

It's the first year with your baby.

By this time, you have settled into your new life. Everything is just how you want it; in fact, it's even better than you could have hoped.

Take a moment to simply stop and notice what you see. Use all your senses, not only what it looks like but what smells, sounds, tastes, and sensations are also present.

Where are you?

Who else is there?

What are you doing?

How do you feel?

Look around this place. Get a complete sense of it. Notice all details.

_____

Now, see yourself moving into another scene from your new life. Here there are different people, or maybe you are alone. Realize that everything is positively ideal. Take as much time as you need to let this new scene emerge.

Notice your surroundings, the energy, how you appear. Notice how you feel.

Where are you now?

Are you alone or are there others around?

What are you doing?

How do you feel in this scene?

_____

Now, see yourself moving into yet another moment of your life—a third scene. Once again, take a moment to simply observe.

What do you see this time?

_____

In the next few minutes, visit other scenes from your life. Spend time in each one, pausing to experience it fully.

Freely wander around. See the different places, activities, and people that fill your days.

Go where your baby is happiest.

Find where you feel most fully yourself and most fully alive.

See the people who are most important to you that first year.

Finally, see yourself on your baby's first birthday. There you are, a woman who is also a mother, reflecting back on that first year. How do you feel at this point in your life? What milestones did you reach? What are you proud of? What did you do to create this feeling of confidence, relaxation, and satisfaction?

When you are ready, see yourself walking back into the room where you are now. Mentally return to the present, feeling alert and rested, and open to any insights that may come.

- **Thinking about your vision.** The gems in visualization are not only what you see, but also what they mean to you. Reflect on your vision. This is not like dream interpretation where certain symbols and actions are "supposed" to mean something specific. There is no right answer. Listen to yourself to find what your visualization means *to you*. Go through the following questions:

  ❷ Look back at where you were and what you were doing. What does this say about your personality and what's important to you?

  ❷ What's new in this life? What surprised you?

  ❷ What did you bring with you from your present-day life? What was the same?

  ❷ What was missing in the vision you saw? What do you make of that absence?

  ❷ What role did money or your career play in your dream?

  ❷ How do you interpret the colors, smells, or sounds in your dream? The actions, locations, and environment?

  ❷ What other interpretations or insights can you draw from your vision?

  Be sure to capture the essence of your visualization in "My Vision" in the "Keepsakes" section in Appendix A.

Exercise 2: Adding to Your Wish List

You will add to the mini wish list that you started earlier. Make sure you are ready for brainstorming and in an open frame of mind before you start dreaming about everything that would make your experience of becoming a mother ideal!

- **Gathering your materials.** Collect everything you need so you can immerse yourself in the process. You might include notes from your exploration in the last chapter, whatever you're going to write on and write with, and anything else you need to be creative.

- **Making wishes.** Keep in mind that you are only collecting ideas when making a wish list. You are not making decisions or even organizing your thoughts. This is brainstorming. Write down anything and everything that comes to mind. The result should be one giant assembly of words, phrases, and images that represent all the possibilities for your first year as a mother.

Use the categories below to stretch your thinking into new areas. Represent your whole life in all its richness on the paper.

- My New Baby
- My Kids (if you have other children)
- My Husband or Partner
- Family
- Friends
- Maternity Leave
- Child Care
- Body and Health
- Home Environment
- Money
- Passion, Calling, or Life Purpose
- Career
- Personal Growth and Spirituality
- Fun and Relaxation

- **Stepping back.** When you have brainstormed all of your ideas for your ideal first year, take a step back and see what they have to teach you. What do you notice as you look at your list? What themes have emerged? What surprises does it offer? Did you find any big ah-ha ideas? Let the thoughts settle and your mind clear. Don't feel you have to rush to organize these thoughts, add to them, delete them, share them, or in any other way edit what you've written. Simply let them be and take the wisdom your wish list offers.

Be sure to document key thoughts and ideas in "My Vision" in the "Keepsakes" section in Appendix A.

Exercise 3: Creating a Quick Collage

A collage isn't just a grade school art project. It's also a way to tap into your intuition and see your vision from yet another angle.

- **Gathering your materials.** Collect a short stack of your favorite magazines. Get a variety if you can—maybe a news weekly, a women's circular, a parenting magazine, and a specialty publication for your hobby or passion.

- **Having fun!** Give yourself a specific amount of time to leaf through the magazines and tear out anything you like. Ten minutes works well—you should move quickly. Give your intuition room to play. Don't censor, don't judge, and don't waver. Just pull out what grabs you.

- **Making your picture.** Now, in whatever sloppy, artistic, balanced, or outlandish way you like, place the pictures all over to create your collage. If you like, you can tape or glue the pictures together, or you can simply use the floor or table as a canvas for a temporary assortment of images representing your new life.

- **Looking for meaning.** Step back and take a good look. What do you see? Notice colors, images, words, objects, environments, and juxtapositions. Ask yourself: What do I think this means? What do I see of myself in this picture? What do I see of my new life?

Be sure to note your insights in "My Vision" in the "Keepsakes" section in Appendix A.

Lessons in BECOMING A MOTHER

Lesson 2 **Mother's Intuition**

Listen to your truth.

Mother's intuition—that inexplicable sixth sense mothers have for instinctively *knowing*—is legendary. Your intuition is the voice that whispers softly what you know to be true, deep down. It's the niggling thought in the back of your mind. Whenever you feel something "in your gut," know it "in your heart," or find yourself exclaiming, "I *knew* it!" your intuition is at work. Intuition is a way of knowing with certainty but without explanation. Although it is not always rational or logical, this inner voice can be a source of immeasurable wisdom.

Your intuition can be invaluable as you envision your new life as a mother. It can help you discover what you really want, clarify your hopes and dreams, and reveal your expectations. Your intuition can also help you resolve some of the big questions of motherhood. (Do I want that big promotion before the baby is born? Should I start remodeling the bathroom now? Is this a good time to switch doctors?)

You don't have to wait to be a mother to tap into your intuition. It's available to everyone when you stop to listen, watch for clues, and notice the messages around you.

Stopping to Listen

The secret to identifying your intuition is to listen closely. Like a radio station that is constantly available if you only tune in, your intuition is always there. You can access it by

- Sitting quietly and clearing your mind.
- Taking several deep breaths to relax.
- Asking your question.
- Paying attention to what your intuition offers.

Intuition cannot be forced. You must extend your intuition an invitation, welcome it, and give it space. Meditation, writing, and quiet time all make it possible for intuition to emerge.

Trying to identify your intuition can be perplexing when you are unable to distinguish between your inner wisdom and the other voices in your head—the "shoulds" and "have tos" of life. Stress, exhaustion, and fear create noise and make it hard to hear your intuition speak. Second-guessing yourself or overanalyzing your thoughts can also get you off track. When seeking your truth, find a calm, relaxed space and just listen for your authentic voice.

Watching for Clues

Intuition isn't always obvious. It can be veiled, indirect, subtle, teasing, or symbolic. It could be an image that pops into your head or the person who showed up in your dream last night. Some people would say it is your unconscious speaking. Other people say it's the universe trying to get your attention. However you describe it, it is the little things that we often ignore that can be our intuition raising its hand, waiting to speak.

Before Denise got pregnant, her life was a whirlwind. Flying all over the country, working twelve-plus hours a day, she and her husband definitely wanted to have kids someday, but the subject hadn't come up in awhile. Then Denise started noticing baby ads on TV and in her magazines. She caught herself smiling at a display in a baby store window and found a dropped child's toy on the ground. It was getting weird. Finally, a pregnant woman sat down next to her on the plane. "Okay, I get the message!" she chuckled. Soon after, she and her husband started talking more seriously about having a baby.

Intuition leaves clues. Learning to be aware of them can help you access your inner truth.

Interpreting the Message

Your intuition gives you information. It's up to you to interpret what it means. Sometimes the meaning is clear, other times not.

For example, for her vision of her ideal first year, Bianca made a sort of collage. She tore out pages from old catalogs and fanned them out around her on the floor. After twenty minutes of tearing out images she liked, she paused and looked around. She had chosen a picture of a mother playing with her child in a big yard, multiple generations sitting around the dinner table, and a family watching the snow fall through a window. She was somewhat surprised by her choices because she lived in a small downtown condo, her parents and in-laws lived on the east coast, and she was in snow-free southern California! Bianca realized that she was envisioning a life similar to her childhood. A few years later when she and her husband moved to Virginia, she said, "I didn't realize when I was pregnant how strong that vision was. All those feelings gelled when Paul was born and prompted the whole move to be closer to our families."

You'd be surprised how many answers you really have about the questions you might be asking. Whether your intuition comes to you or you go chasing after it, it can be a window into your heart—and your future.

CHAPTER THREE

Step 3
CLARIFYING YOUR VALUES

*"We make our future dreams come true
by acting on our values today."*
—*Marvin Weisbord*

In motherhood, it can be hard to see where you're going. You might not feel like you know what you're doing. You might be afraid of what's ahead, and you might be freaked out by what's happening now. Sometimes the way can seem dark.

Your values will illuminate your new life.

In this chapter, you will discover the very essence of *you*—the values that characterize you and who you will be as a woman *and* as a mother. Your values can be a steadfast guiding force in your life as you navigate your way through the twists and turns of life with a baby.

Building a Solid Foundation

To start creating a foundation for motherhood, you will identify your core values. Your values are the principles, standards, and qualities that keep you centered and bring you fulfillment. Values describe the heart of what life is for you.

To understand the concept of values, it's helpful to know what a value is and is not. Think of it this way: If you can see it, feel it, or touch it, it's not a value but the expression of a value. A value is the experience behind those things that gives them worth. Here are some examples.

- Material goods are not values. Money may be important to you, but money is not a value. What is it about money that you most value? Security? Freedom? Pleasure? Now, those are potential values.

- Concrete objects and people are not values. Your friends may be important to you, but a friend is not a value. What is it about your friends that you value? Belonging? Laughter? Support? Again, these are possible values.

- Goals are not values. Even though you might want to lose weight, being a certain dress size is not a value. It's a goal. The value behind it might be confidence or good health or beauty (or it just might be a fear in disguise).

Expectations, material objects, people, goals, and even fears can masquerade as values and send you down the wrong path.

A value is intangible. It is a principle, standard, or quality. It is not a concrete object or person. A value is something you can embrace, not attain. You will be able to express and experience your values in a wide variety of circumstances. Values are expansive, not limiting. None of those things are true for objects, people, and goals, which are specific, focused, and concrete. Take a look at the sample list of values to get a better sense of what they are.

SAMPLE VALUES

Trust	Faith	Service	Caring	Compassion
Relationship	Quality of Life	Health	Achievement	Authenticity
Wellness	Renewal	Freedom	Beauty	Integrity
Learning	Growth	Fun	Choice	Security
Joy	Gratitude	Outer Peace	Inner Peace	Honesty
Generosity	Adventure	Order	Abundance	Spirituality
Audacity	Impact	Intensity	Simplicity	Harmony
Clarity	Frugality	Independence	Discovery	Love
Acceptance	Wisdom	Creativity	Imagination	Forgiveness
Balance	Courage	Truth	Delight	Pleasure
Accomplishment	Respect	Courtesy	Openness	Power

Defining your values can be a simple task or an involved process. Some women are already quite clear on their values. Others have never given it much thought. Identifying your values means asking yourself what's really important in your life—what brings life meaning, richness, and fulfillment—and listing those things clearly and succinctly so you can refer to them as a guide for your life.

Living Your Values

Many women find that motherhood changes them. Their priorities shift; they see the world differently. Every aspect of their identity can be touched, from their career to their appearance to their relationships.

For many women, the change that overcomes them when entering motherhood is inspiring and joyful. For others, it's frightening or even depressing. To make new motherhood the most positive experience possible, you need to feel solid in the knowledge of who you really are even if your world is in upheaval. You need to be clear on what you care about most *before* your baby is born so you don't lose touch with it afterwards. In other words, you need to know your core values.

As a first-time mother, you may not know much about babies, but you can know a whole a lot about yourself. Being clear about your values will keep you grounded and help guide your decisions. Although the specific things that are important to you may change after your baby is born, your values endure. For instance, you may have always expressed your value for health by hitting the gym every morning. After the baby arrives, you may express that same value a different way, perhaps by getting enough sleep or choosing your foods more carefully. You can honor your values even if you express them differently in your new life. This way, you keep your identity and maintain what is core to your happiness while at the same time welcoming in your new baby. We call this *living your values*.

Living in sync with your values is key to fulfillment and contentment. In order to live your values, you need to get to know them, understand what they mean to you, and remember them so you can stay true to yourself. As a result, you can give more to your baby without giving away your self.

"I've been wanting to paint a mural in the baby's room but it's always the last thing on my list. Remembering that I really value my creativity—darn it, I'm going to find a way to do this!"   —MARSHA, 6 MONTHS PREGNANT

FINDING YOUR OWN WAY
Identifying Your Values

You are now about to identify the specific values that will ensure fulfillment and contentment in your new life. We will ask you several questions to help clarify your values, then we will provide additional suggestions and details in "A Closer Look." Your end result will be a list of seven core values with personal definitions uniquely suited to you. Your values are the first component of your "Foundation for Motherhood," which you will find in the "Keepsakes" section at the end of this book. Notice that your foundation includes your values, beliefs, and intention, all of which you will be creating in this and the next two chapters. We call it your foundation because it will keep you strong and steady, and you will refer back to it over and over for the rest of your life.

Get your pen and your journal or a piece a paper. Ask yourself:

What's most important to me in the first year of motherhood?

Now start collecting possibilities. Don't worry about finding the exact right values or whether what you identified counts as a value. Write down whatever springs to mind. Think back to your exploration and vision from the previous two chapters for more ideas. Don't censor anything; all your ideas are fine as they are.

When you've had a chance to generate some ideas, ask yourself this question:

What values do I see behind the ideas on my list?

Write them down! If you need help remembering what a value looks like, go back to the sample list of values earlier in this chapter.

You might need to practice finding the values within your ideas. Some values are easy to spot. For example, Sophie wrote that the health and safety of her baby was important in the first year as well as keeping her own mind and body healthy. Clearly, "health" was a potential value for Sophie. Other values are harder to discern. Jade recalled the vision of her ideal first year—a scene where she took a long walk on the beach with her baby. She saw many values in this picture such as "beauty," "joy," and "serenity." Indeed, she did value all these qualities, but when Jade reflected on the scene, she realized that being *alone* on the beach with her baby was the appealing part. She wrote down "solitude" as her potential value.

Once you have a list of several potential values, the next step is to personalize them so each value comes alive. Take one of your potential values and think about what makes that quality specific to *you*. If "joy" is on your list, is this the kind of joy that comes from watching a spectacular sunrise, the joy of zooming off on your bike for the first time, or the joy of laughing hysterically with a girlfriend? Maureen's version of joy was captured in her vision of the first year, "I picture my baby in the bath. Water is splashing me. There are squishy bath toys and such joy on my baby's face." Maureen decided to call her value "splashy joy" so she could remember exactly what she needed in her life as she became a mother. Look at your list and describe your values in your own words.

To finalize your list, choose seven to be your core values. We recommend seven so you have enough to represent the diversity of who you are but not too many to keep top of mind. You may even want to order them, with the most crucial value first. Discovering your values is a process that requires effort and discernment. You most likely will want to spend more time refining your list. Remember there are additional suggestions in "A Closer Look" to help you complete your list.

Once you know your values, you can bring them into your life right away. Many women post their values on a wall or at their desk. Some choose to make a formal version with a symbol or picture to illustrate each value. Sharing your values also brings them into your life. Sit down and show them to your husband or partner and invite him to do the same! As you move into motherhood, see how you can honor your values each day.

KEEPSAKE

Write down the seven values you chose in the "My Foundation for Motherhood" worksheet in the "Keepsakes" section in Appendix A or in your own journal or notebook.

TIPS FOR CLARIFYING YOUR VALUES

- Dig to find the values that are most important to you.
- Remember, a value is not a "thing" but a principle, standard, or quality.
- Spend the time to personalize your values.
- Go easy—let your values be a work in progress.
- Make your values a part of your life—keep them in view.

"Taking the time to clearly define my values was critical for me. I see it as a way of connecting the old me to the new me."   —URSULA, 6 MONTHS PREGNANT

Common Experiences _____

Discovering your values can be an eye-opening experience. Seeing them in black and white on the page can be like emerging from a fog as the most meaningful components of your life appear before you in sparkling clarity. The right list of values is clean, pure truth—truth about who you are and what matters in your life. Of course, it is only the beginning of a journey in which you will start to form your life around those values, but it is a key step.

As you search for your values, several things may happen. Here are some experiences shared by other expecting mothers.

Realizing You're Not Honoring Your Values. You might discover a latent value that you're not currently honoring. When Jessica sat down to ask herself about her values, the word that popped into her head was "spirituality." It rang like a bell, and Jessica immediately wrote it down as her number one value. But what struck her next was even more significant: Nowhere in her life was she actually expressing her spirituality. She hadn't been attending church as she used to, reading the books that inspired her, writing in her journal, meditating—nothing. Jessica was confronted with the disconnect between her values and her reality. Often, recognizing this kind of incongruence can prompt a realignment of priorities.

Being Influenced by "Shoulds." Some moms-to-be find that looking for their values feels forced or superficial at first. Years and years of living have taught us what the "right" answers are—what's "supposed" to be important in our lives. You may want to test the values you identify for a while to see if they're really authentic. Maybe you know you should value "family," but the time you feel most whole and rewarded is when you're alone in the tub, or in the spotlight at work, or skiing down a mountain with your girlfriends. Allow yourself to be open to what your values actually are, not what you think they should be.

Knowing What You Don't Want. Sometimes it's easier to identify what you *don't* want in your life than what you *do* want. That can also be a start for finding your values. Carole, for instance, cringed when she thought of the pressure her tendency toward perfectionism could bring after her baby was born. She searched for the opposite of perfectionism for a value that made her feel at ease: "learning and accepting who I am." Carole also wanted to move away from excessively questioning herself and her ability to be a good mother, so she chose a value about trusting herself. She also recognized a fear of feeling isolated and created a value around relationships and support. Notice that in this process, Carole was actually making up her values as she went along, choosing what she wanted to be most important to her instead of what had held her hostage in the past.

Getting Creative. The fun part about finding your values is that they are so specific to *you*. As in so many steps along the road to becoming a mother, you get to play! The values you come up with may not be the typical ones like "health," "relationships," or "achievement." Notice how some of these expecting found creative names for their values, and how much more personal these values became.

"Healthy boundaries." For this mom-to-be, healthy boundaries meant giving herself space to allow for personal growth.

"Authentic achievement." The woman who identified this value was expressing her desire to make a contribution and to be more of herself at work and at home.

"Lighten up!" This expecting mother's value reminded her to smile, have fun, feel joy, and take pleasure in life.

To personalize your values so that they truly reflect who you are, keep asking yourself what it is you care about, in your own words. Then use those words to form the name of a value that speaks to you.

Feeling Transformed. The process of clarifying values can be positively transformational. It's powerful to write down your values, list them, and claim them as your own. So, watch out—this exercise can be life changing.

Many of the mothers we know have made changes right away to better honor their values before their babies arrived. You may be able to do this fairly easily, as Carole did. She wanted to practice living her values while she was still pregnant. She knew her tendency toward perfectionism would compromise the kind of motherhood she wanted. She challenged herself to start working on the issue by honoring her value of self-acceptance. She worked at this little by little—at her job and at home—even in small ways like "not needing to have *everything* in the bathroom put away where it belongs." Or you may find that practicing your values is a bigger challenge, as Leslie did. "My favorite value is one I call 'vital engagement.' To me it means no holding back. It's unreserved loving. It's easy to see how I want to bring that to my baby. What is harder is how might I practice it with my husband or, even more tricky, with myself."

It may seem that honoring your values should be easy and natural, since values reflect what's most important in your life. But it takes practice and awareness. If your goal is to become a mother without losing your self, start living your values *now*.

A Light to Lead Your Way

It's easy to get lost in new motherhood. With so much changing around you, with plenty to learn and do, with some confusion and occasional dark moments, it helps to have a light to lead the way. Your values provide that light.

In this chapter, you have identified core values you want to guide your life and personalized those values so you know exactly what they mean. By naming your values, you have connected deeply with what matters most to you. This is a significant step forward toward the fulfillment and contentment that characterize your ideal first year as a mother.

You are already forming your identity as a new mother. No matter what happens after your baby arrives, from explosive diapers to explosive emotions, your values will help you find your way.

How do I live my values today?

C O N G R A T U L A T I O N S !

You have just completed a list of your core values for your new life. We want to acknowledge you for

- Looking deeply beneath the surface of your life to see what's important to you.
- Sifting through the possibilities to learn what makes you unique.
- Claiming your values.
- Starting to lay the foundation for your motherhood.

A Closer Look

In the chapter, you started searching for you values. The exercise below helps you find more places to look and suggestions to refine and complete your list of values.

Exercise: Completing Your List of Values

If you really want to feel secure in your values, you must do enough investigating to uncover all the possibilities, refine them, and feel certain about the core values you choose.

- **Finding more possibilities.** There are endless places to look for your values. Try thinking of times in your life where you were exhilarated, challenged, or taken to the edge—a peak moment. What about that moment most strikes you? Write down your thoughts.

    Think about something that scares you about motherhood or something you *don't* want. What is being threatened in that scenario? What are you afraid of losing? There is usually an important value lurking in these places.

    Additional places to look are your favorite possessions, most admired people, music and art that you love, or the food you most passionately crave. What is it about these people, places, or things that grabs you? Every time you expose a value, write it down.

- **Locating the values.** Among the words you are creating, you will have some values and some that are simply descriptions. Pick out the values you see already written on the page, like "love," "growth," or "authenticity." Circle them.

    Now look at what's left and dig for the values beneath the words. You might have written "sailing with my husband" as a peak moment. The underlying value might be "passion and connection" or "fun and light-heartedness." If you wrote my "my corner office" as one of your favorite things, you might identify values like "security," "achievement," and "respect." If you wrote that you don't want a crying baby

EXTRA RESOURCES

An attractive electronic version of your "Foundation for Motherhood" worksheet is available at **www.empoweredmotherhood.com**. You can post it on a bulletin board or fridge as a lasting reminder of what's most important to you!

because you are worried that you won't know what to do, look at what's at stake. Is it your sense of competence? Your image? Your baby's safety? Note any values you find.

- **Refining your values.** Add to, edit, refine, and condense your list. Do you see some repeats? Are there themes? Play with the words, combining some that seem similar, adding any that are missing, deleting any that no longer feel important, and changing the words to accurately reflect what you mean.

- **Personalizing your values.** Remember you can be creative with this list! To personalize your values, use words that you love, phrases that speak to you, and unique ideas. It doesn't matter that no one else knows what you mean when you have a value called "belly laughs" or "it's not rocket science" or "magical moments." What matters is that they mean something to you.

Personalize each value and then define it. The value of "creativity" may mean painting to one woman, wearing eclectic clothes combinations to someone else, or brainstorming clever ideas for another. Create your own definition that captures the essence of your value and write it down in a sentence or two by each value. This is where the values become *yours* instead of just a list of words.

- **Choosing your core values.** Choose no more than seven values that are closest to your heart. These are the ones that you can build your life around. Remember to share your values with your husband or partner, put them up where you can see them, and start honoring them in your everyday life.

Be sure to write down your values in "My Foundation for Motherhood" in the "Keepsakes" section in Appendix A.

Lessons in BECOMING A MOTHER

Lesson 3 Values-Centered Living

Use your values to guide your daily actions and decisions.

When you're a mother, your values take on a new importance—not just philosophically, but in a very practical way. Applying your values can streamline, energize, and enrich your everyday life.

Streamlining

By living your values, you streamline your life. No matter how busy, stressed out, or confused you are, your values can bring you instant clarity. All you need to do is to ask this one question: "If I were to honor my values, what would I decide or do?"

Here's an example. Reva was a graphic artist in a busy firm who felt positively frenetic in her last few months of pregnancy. As her maternity leave grew nearer and nearer, her task list grew longer and longer. With four weeks to go, Reva finally had to admit there was no way she could do it all. But she also didn't know how to stop.

Reva asked herself the question, "What would I do if I were to honor my values?"

Immediately, she saw a new path. Two of Reva's top values were "devotion" and "creative expression." Together, these two values directed Reva to dedicate all of her time to completing projects for her most cherished clients. She was flooded with energy and enthusiasm as she realized she could spend the last month of her pregnancy doing exactly what she loved! Reva could stop working on the corporate planning project that she had taken on in an effort to impress her boss. She could give away the new proposals that she wouldn't be able to work on anyway once her maternity leave started. She could give up the paperwork, the politics, and the projects she'd said "yes" to just because she couldn't say "no." Instead, she could finish one client's new brochure, launch another's campaign, and complete the website for a third—work she loved to do and would get her clients the best possible results. Reva's values focused her on what really mattered. Everything else fell away.

Energizing

Your values can breathe energy into almost any mundane or trivial task. All it takes is connecting the task back to your values. Instead of asking, "How will I ever get this done?" you can ask, "What's the value in doing this?"

For instance, Yuchin was procrastinating filling out a stack of health insurance forms to clear up a billing error. When she answered the question, "What's the value in doing this?" her perspective shifted. "This is about our health! Our safety! Our security!" Her values reminded her that although she dreaded the paperwork, the reasons for getting through it affected basic aspects of her life. Yuchin rode on the fresh surge of energy, finished the forms, and mailed them that day!

You can find your values in almost any chore. What's the value in cooking dinner tonight? Nurturing yourself and your family, providing a center point around which to connect. What's the value in sorting through all those baby hand-me-downs? Being economical and grateful. What's the value in those endless trips to the doctor? Protecting your baby and caring for yourself. Whatever task you're resisting, your values can put the noble back in the mundane—providing motivation and momentum.

Enriching

In addition to helping you prioritize what to do and giving you energy to do it, your values also help you see *how* to approach each moment. Using your values enables you to make each moment rich and full. That's no small feat for busy mothers who often are hurrying to get everything done and feeling guilty that they aren't doing it better. The question is, "How do I approach this if I am faithful to my values?"

Julie's values became particularly helpful after her baby was born. She worked from home one day a week to save on commuting costs and to spend more time with her son Nathan. Even so, Julie felt incredibly guilty when she sat down to work, leaving Nathan with the sitter. However, she also felt she was ignoring her work when playing with Nathan. Julie's work-from-home day usually felt pressured and disjointed. Finally, she turned to her values.

One of Julie's values was "full-circle graciousness"—her own expression to represent the importance of both giving and receiving. Julie asked herself, "How do I approach working at home if I'm faithful to full-circle graciousness?" This value reminded Julie that she could give love and attention to her baby, but she also could graciously receive time and focus for her work. Julie set up a routine in which every morning before opening her email and every afternoon after shutting off her laptop, she gave Nathan undivided attention. This small shift helped Julie drop the guilt and be more generous with herself and her son.

Living your values can redefine the fundamental tasks of new motherhood—feeding, sleeping, discipline, playing, and housework. They can show you where to put your energy, who to spend time with, what to expose your child to, and how to treat yourself.

CHAPTER FOUR

Step 4
CHOOSING YOUR BELIEFS

"Live your beliefs and you can turn the world around."
—Henry David Thoreau

Beliefs are a powerful force in our lives. Yet beliefs are often adopted by default. Parents, friends, the media, religion, spirituality, politics, and life experiences all contribute to the way a person sees the world. Many people never stop to consider what their beliefs actually *are;* they just go around assuming "this is the way life is."

A more conscious way of living is to examine your beliefs, recognize their influence on your life, and change them to align them with your values.

In this chapter, we walk you through that process. You will be considering the beliefs you hold about motherhood and comparing them to other possibilities. Ultimately, we help you prepare a set of beliefs that will guide you into motherhood with clarity and confidence.

Limiting and Empowering Beliefs

You get to consciously choose your beliefs for new motherhood. Some beliefs might empower you, while others could limit you. By becoming aware of your beliefs, you can keep the ones that serve you, weed out the ones that don't, and choose the ones that will support who you want to be. Throughout this process, you clarify your view of the world to see if it helps build the life you want.

Here's an example. A common belief of expectant mothers is, "My husband or partner won't be as important to me after the baby arrives." Can you imagine the effects of this belief on a relationship? A woman with this belief may actually diminish her partnership so that she can fully step into her new role as a mother—and do so at a time when that relationship matters most. Such a limiting belief assumes a woman cannot be *both* a valuable contributor to her personal relationship *and* a whole-hearted mother. The belief forces her to choose one role *over* the other. It automatically limits her ability to fulfill different parts of herself.

Now consider this belief instead: "Having a baby will create a radical new connection with my partner." This belief is so much more empowering! It opens up possibilities. It still accepts the potential for change once the baby is born, but it does so with a note of excitement. This belief makes it not only possible for a mother to be a great partner, but gives her a chance to be better at both.

Beliefs are fundamental to the way your life plays out. The difference between a limiting and an empowering belief is quite literally the difference between a limited and a powerful life. Choose your beliefs carefully. They make you who you are.

> *"I am bombarded with other people's beliefs about how having a baby will affect my life. People keep telling me, 'Your life is going to change,' or 'You'd better go on vacation now, you'll never have time after the baby,' and 'You'll never be alone with your husband again,' as if this is the only way things could be. It's a relief to stop and consider what I choose to think."* —TANYA, 8 MONTHS PREGNANT

Separating Facts from Opinions

Motherhood is full of beliefs, and it can become pretty confusing. Whether you're choosing cloth or disposable diapers, debating approaches for how to get your baby to sleep through the night, or thinking about the effect working would have on your life and baby, everyone will have a belief about which way is "right."

That can create a lot of pressure, unless you realize that beliefs are only opinions. Beliefs are not facts, even though they're often expressed as though they are. Take a look at the facts and beliefs below and notice the difference.

Here is a fact: Babies require time to get into a rhythm of sleeping, waking, and eating. Here are three related, but disputable, beliefs:

Belief: Mothers should put their babies on a schedule from day one.

Belief: Mothers should gradually introduce their babies to a routine.

Belief: Mothers should let their babies find their own routine.

These beliefs are hotly disputed, and you can find people who believe each one strongly.

Here is another example. This is a fact: Babies need love and nurturing to thrive. Again, here are some related beliefs:

Belief: No one will take care of your baby as well as you can.

Belief: A well-rested friend or family member can take better care of a baby at the moment if the mother is feeling frazzled and worn out.

Belief: Babies can be happy in anyone's arms, as long as they feel safe and secure.

These three beliefs contradict each other, but they all support the facts.

Look how the beliefs oppose each other, yet each one comes across with conviction. Once you realize that the ideas most people present to you are beliefs, not facts, you are free to choose your *own* beliefs based on the facts and your own way of thinking.

Experts, authors, and mothers from every generation surround you, and they've all been through what you've been through—or so they think. The difference is, they went through it in their way, based on their beliefs. What they believe—as well as what they thought, what they did, and inevitably what they think you should do—may not be right for you. While it is helpful to have the experience of others to draw from, you have a right to do things your way.

If you don't consciously choose your beliefs—just like if you're not clear about your values—you can be easily swayed and end up making decisions based on what's right for somebody else. That's why it's important to recognize beliefs for what they are: different perspectives or points of view. You can think them over, weigh them, and decide if you agree. When you know your beliefs, you can confront opposing beliefs with grace. You can consider them, but not necessarily adopt them. You can understand them without agreeing with them. You can reject them without feeling guilty. There is a great sense of peace that comes from knowing and basing decisions on beliefs you have chosen—not the ones imposed on you from everyone else.

> *"For months after my first son was born, I was going nearly insane reading books about how to care for a baby. This one said feed on demand, that one said set a schedule; this one said be flexible, that one said be vigilant. It was only when I figured out that these were all just theories—conflicting theories—that I was able to free myself up to figure out what was best for me. At that point I could read the advice more objectively, searching for what I agreed with and what I didn't, instead of feeling lectured by 'experts' who knew more than I did."*   —LAURA, MOTHER OF TWO

FINDING YOUR OWN WAY:
Making Your Beliefs

It's time for you to be honest about what you currently believe and what you *want* to believe. You will choose your beliefs about motherhood so that you, and nobody else, will lead your life as a mother. We offer ideas and questions to help you clarify your beliefs, then provide more detailed suggestions under "A Closer Look." Ultimately, you will choose five beliefs to add to your "Foundation for Motherhood" in the "Keepsakes" section of the book.

Start by asking yourself:

❓ What makes a good mother?

Think about all the different answers that come to mind as you ask yourself that question. What voices do you hear? Your mother? Husband or partner? Friends? The media? Sift through the different beliefs and pick one for the moment that resonates.

State that belief assertively—say it aloud right now, testing it out to be sure it's what you really believe. Now, imagine declaring this belief to everyone you know from your husband or partner, to your mother-in-law, to your future pediatrician, to your co-workers, to your best friend. As you do this, notice how you feel in each circumstance. Are there any moments in which you feel a twinge of discomfort? A little shame? Some embarrassment? Those are signs that something is misaligned—either that you're not being honest about what *you* really believe or that your belief is significantly different from someone else's.

Look for a positive response. Do you feel comfortable and settled? Proud? Confident? You might experience a gut level reaction when your belief feels intuitively right. Those are signs that you have struck a belief that rings true for you.

Finding an authentic belief requires patience. For example, Katie answered "What makes a good mother?" with "Fulfilling myself in my career so that I can feel complete inside; then I will be a stronger mother for my baby." As committed as Katie felt when she spoke that belief to herself, she started shrinking as she imagined sharing it with others. She predicted her friend Karen, a stay-at-home mother who had left her career as an elementary schoolteacher, would either feel judged by Katie's belief or would lash out that it wasn't true.

Imagining the conversation that would ensue, Katie began to feel guilty. "Maybe it's selfish of me to believe that," she wondered. "Maybe I just *want* to believe that it's true, because I don't want to give up my career." As she continued to imagine stating her belief to different people, she realized that imagining sharing it with her boss made her feel strong and alive, but imaging sharing it with her mother made her feel meek like a little girl. Katie constantly kept asking herself, is this what I *really* believe?

Katie started to see that her original belief was limiting the way she saw herself and the possibilities for her new life. If she fully adopted the belief, it meant that she *had* to work to feel fulfilled. The part of her that was a career woman vehemently agreed. The part of her that was raised by a stay-at-home mother did not. Katie searched for a belief that felt good on her tongue and in her heart. Ultimately, Katie created a new belief: "A good mother *is fulfilled as a person*, however she might gain that fulfillment." Katie didn't know if working would continue to fulfill her or not after her baby was born. What she did know was that she had pinpointed a belief that made her feel confident—a belief she could truly base her life on.

Questioning your beliefs about motherhood can highlight conflicts, both internal and external. Use this is as an opportunity for self-growth and learning more about the people in your life. Be curious about your husband's or partner's beliefs about parenthood. See if those beliefs conflict with, align, or complement yours.

The process of distilling your beliefs is not black and white. Allow yourself time to try on different beliefs and see what fits and what doesn't. Notice when you feel limited and deflated, and when you feel expansive and energized. Keep working with the wording of your beliefs until you've created the ones that you can claim with conviction—the beliefs that will help you be the woman and mother *you* really want to be. We suggest you choose five beliefs to use as you go through the process in this book. There are more questions to help you choose your beliefs in "A Closer Look."

KEEPSAKE

Write down the five beliefs you chose in "My Foundation for Motherhood" in the "Keepsakes" section in Appendix A or in your own journal or notebook.

TIPS FOR CHOOSING YOUR BELIEFS

- Focus on finding beliefs that will help you move past fear and limitations.
- Let go of old default beliefs.
- Try on different beliefs until you find those that fit.
- Embrace and share the beliefs you choose.

Common Experiences _____

Examining beliefs can send you all over the map emotionally. It can be a process of moving from being unaware of what you believe, to being hyper-aware of what you believe, to experimenting with the wording of beliefs to find the one that fits. Below we share some of the experiences of other women who have gone through this process.

Collaborating with Others. Some mothers need a partner to help find their beliefs. It's like shopping for the perfect shoes: Sometimes you need your best friend to give you her opinion, even if you don't end up taking her advice. It can be helpful to bounce ideas off other people to tease out your beliefs.

For instance, Franca talked to her husband Brett about different beliefs. Together they noticed that many of their beliefs were arbitrarily based on how their friends were parenting and living with children. Franca and Brett spent most of their conversation choosing new beliefs that reflected their own particular values and hopes for the kind of life they envisioned for their family.

Similarly, Amanda had trouble pinpointing her own beliefs by herself. She needed help to uncover them. She started asking other people what *they* thought made a good mother and listened with genuine interest. Along the way, she turned the ideas over in her head. "Do I agree with that?" she asked herself over and over. "Does that belief limit or empower me?" After a few weeks of exploring the question in this way, she felt clearer on which beliefs suited her and which ones didn't.

Beliefs are so embedded in our thinking that it can be difficult to see them by ourselves. Sometimes we're simply too close to them to be able differentiate our opinions from facts. This is a great time to work with a coach, a mentor, or a friend who can help point out and examine your beliefs.

Rooting out Fear. Investigating beliefs can bring fears to the surface. Fears can actually become rooted in beliefs, making them very powerful indeed. For instance, when Bea started exploring her beliefs, she uncovered some fears lurking underneath.

"I don't deserve motherhood."

"My baby won't love me that much."

"The baby will be a real financial burden and sacrifice for my husband."

"It will be too hard."

Bea had to get these fear-based beliefs out of her system before she could move on to more uplifting ones. "It was really important for me to write them on a piece of paper," she said. "Otherwise I would have been just shoving them down. I couldn't choose new beliefs until I dealt with the ones that were there." Being honest about her beliefs felt liberating because it meant Bea could now choose to change them.

Once Bea had identified her current beliefs, she asked herself this question: "If this is what I *have been believing,* what do I *now want to believe?*" She discovered that more empowering beliefs were perfectly plausible. Thus "I don't deserve motherhood" became "Motherhood is a gift that is mine to open." The belief "The baby will be a burden for my husband" became "Our family has the capacity to change and grow." "It will be too hard" became "I have everything I need to be a great mother. What I don't know, I can learn." Bea felt more self-assured as a result of her process of identifying fear-based beliefs, challenging them, and replacing them with empowering beliefs.

Giving It Time. Assessing every belief you've ever had about motherhood can be an intimidating task, especially because your beliefs are such an embedded part of the way you think. If you put too much pressure on yourself, it can feel heavy. Instead, allow yourself to simply explore and give it time.

Candace's route to a new belief took her five whole years. Even before she got pregnant, she held dear the idea that "if something's worth doing, it's worth doing well." Through coaching and reflection, she came to see that as a limiting belief—one that tied her to excessive attention to quality in even the most trivial of tasks. She wanted to lighten up when she become a new mom. A quotation by consultant Marshall Thurber caught her attention: "Anything worth doing well is worth doing badly in the beginning." This new belief gave her permission to be new at motherhood, even do it badly if she had to at first. Two years later, her belief is shifting again as she is moving to a much softer way of life: "It's only worth doing if it gets you results." She finds this belief gives her the ability to let go of doing a lot of things that don't contribute meaning to her life—leaving her more time for fun with her "baby," who is now 3.

In this chapter, we prompt you to choose five beliefs to support your new life. But this is just a starting point for reflection we hope you will continue. Forming your beliefs is not an exercise but a lifelong endeavor.

Believing in Yourself

There's truth to the idea that anything is possible if you believe. Your beliefs have the power to propel you into an extraordinary life.

You have started the process of examining your beliefs and choosing the ones that will enhance your new life as a mother. You may have confirmed long-held beliefs that have helped to make you the incredible woman you are today. Or, you may have abandoned beliefs that have held you back for years. You may even have chosen new beliefs altogether. You are now becoming aware of ideas that limit and empower you, which will enable you to choose a path to motherhood that aligns with what you want for yourself, your family, and your baby.

You do not have to live according to someone else's rules. Claim your beliefs! It is up to you to direct the course of your life. Ultimately, you are believing in yourself.

What belief will set me free?

C O N G R A T U L A T I O N S !

You have moved deeper into the process of *Becoming a Mother*. We want to acknowledge you for

- Examining and challenging what you think.
- Looking for what empowers you.
- Consciously choosing your own beliefs.
- Creating your own distinctive approach to motherhood.

A Closer Look

Exercise: Completing Your List of Beliefs

Clarifying your beliefs can be a challenge. Here is a more detailed process and examples to help you choose your five beliefs. Take the time to ensure that you have examined the possibilities and choose the most empowering beliefs possible for your new life.

- **Collecting more beliefs.** Getting a sense of what other people think can help you refine and possibly expand your thinking. Explore the questions below to uncover different beliefs about motherhood.

? What are my husband's or partner's beliefs about motherhood?

? What does my mother believe? My mother-in-law?

? My friends?

? Who is a mother that I would like to emulate? What are her beliefs?

? What beliefs does the media portray about motherhood?

? What do I believe about motherhood and how it fits into my life?

Pick up the phone and ask people you know what they believe! Keep in mind that you will *not* be adopting all these beliefs; you are surveying the possibilities to start your process. Jot down your answers as you go.

- **Experimenting with these beliefs.** Look at all the beliefs you've gathered and see what is there. Some beliefs might resonate with you. Other beliefs might have an element of truth, but need rewording. Still others might be the opposite of what you want to believe and need to be turned inside out. Experiment with each belief doing your best to transform it into a positive and personal statement.

For example, Irene asked herself, "Who is a mother that I would like to emulate? What are her beliefs?" Her first response was, "My friend Teri. She loves her children and recognizes them as the exceptional people they are." Irene worked

---

EXTRA RESOURCES

Don't forget to go to **www.empoweredmotherhood.com** for an electronic version of your "Foundation for Motherhood" worksheet!

with the belief to make it her own by using the word "I" and "she" for her baby girl. The result was, "I will love my child and recognize her as the unique person she is."

Another example. In response to the question, "What beliefs does the media portray about motherhood?" Rhonda wrote, "Mothers are perfect." This expectant mother found the opposite to be liberating and created the belief, "Mothers are *not* perfect!"

One more example. Audrey asked herself, "What does my mother think?" After asking her mother, Audrey wrote down, "One learns how to be a mother by doing, not by reading books." She appreciated the sentiment of her mom's belief but wanted to acknowledge her own love of research and studying. Audrey created a belief that really rang true for her. "A woman learns how to be a mother by accessing all her resources and then listening to her heart."

- **Categorizing your beliefs.** For each of the beliefs you have now, ask yourself whether the belief *empowers* you as a mother or *limits* you. What empowers one woman may limit another. Consider this belief: "Motherhood is the most precious role you'll ever have." One woman may find this belief frees her to embrace her new identity as a mother. Another might find it constricting in that it minimizes her other important roles like a wife, community leader, and professional. A perfectly good belief can keep you from where you want to go, especially if it's someone else's belief and not your own. Circle those beliefs that feel empowering to *you*.

- **Refining your beliefs.** Revise the circled beliefs as much or as little as you like until each represents your true conviction. Continue this process until your list contains only empowering beliefs that move you closer to being the woman and mother you want to be.

- **Choosing your beliefs.** Finally, you get to officially choose your beliefs. Look at what you have left on your list. Read each belief out aloud. Which ones appeal to you most? Circle the ones that feel good in your heart and mind—these are the beliefs that will best support you on the path to motherhood.

Be sure to add your beliefs to "My Foundation for Motherhood" in the "Keepsakes" section in Appendix A.

Lessons in BECOMING A MOTHER

Lesson 4 **Handling Judgment**

Stand confident in the face of judgment.

Motherhood can be a divisive issue. Even among mothers. Fortunately or unfortunately, people tend to have strong feelings about motherhood, and they're not always shy about sharing them. The clearer you are about what you believe, the more confident you will feel as a mother. But if you're feeling at all vulnerable (and what new mother doesn't?), even the most well-intentioned judgment can feel like an attack. Maintaining faith in your values, beliefs, and the choices you make is a considerable challenge when you feel that they are questioned.

Feeling judged as a new mother can be unsettling. If you decide to go back to work, there will be friends or family who believe you should be staying home with your baby. If you decide to stay home, there will be someone who thinks you shouldn't give up your career. If you decide to breastfeed, someone will object to you nursing in public, and if you use formula, someone else will say you should nurse. As if having a baby and changing your whole life aren't enough to manage, you have to cope with everyone else's opinions as well. It helps to have a few strategies for handling judgment in your pocket.

Getting Curious

Motherhood can be a humbling experience, full of personal challenges. When you feel judged by other people, remember that they had their challenges, too. Instead of gasping, "I can't believe she said that," you can ask, "I wonder what made her say that?" For instance, the person you're talking to may feel she never had choices in her life and could be speaking out of resentment or regret. Perhaps she did things differently than you, so she thinks what you're doing makes her wrong. Getting curious about other people's experiences can help you see their comments in a different light.

When people confront you with their beliefs, try to see where they could be coming from. This is not the same as feeling pity or judging them back. A good way to handle judgment is to have compassion and forgiveness and then get back to making your life work for you.

Assuming Best Intent

When people tell you what to do, what not to do, or in any way accuse you of not doing something "right," you can detach yourself from the criticism by assuming they mean well. Often, they do.

Take Lauren for instance. Lauren was positively vicious to mothers who didn't correctly strap their babies into car seats, strollers, or grocery carts. As an emergency room doctor, she had seen more injuries and deaths from improper safety than she could count. She may have come across as judgmental, but she merely wanted to save another mother from that pain.

Leslie tended to chide mothers whose babies didn't sleep through the night. Even though she came across as judgmental, she really meant to be helpful. She had been very successful getting her twins to sleep and felt so much better when she did that she wanted other mothers to get the same relief.

No matter where you stand with respect to motherhood, there's always another point of view. If you can assume the best about people's intentions, you're less likely to feel judged yourself.

Speaking Your Truth

Standing strong in the face of judgment requires you to speak your truth. *You* know whose best interest you have at heart. *You* know what's best for you. When other people question your decisions, thoughts, or plans, you can return to your values and beliefs. Simply remembering them can help you ward off unwelcome opinions. You can share your thoughts with others to help them see why you've made the choices you have. Just don't be attached to their approval.

Sharing decisions might sound something like these statements below.

- Imagine someone is pressuring you to join a committee. You say, "Family life is one of my highest values. I'm choosing to spend more time with my child now instead of taking on new commitments."

- Imagine someone is questioning the way you are feeding your baby. You say, "I believe in the benefits of nursing, and it's something I want to do for my daughter," or, "Nursing wasn't right for us, and I believe that what's most important is that my son is healthy and loved."

- Imagine someone is questioning your decision about working after the baby is born. You say, "It's important to me to grow in my career as I grow in my personal life. I'm looking for a way to balance both that honors my professional life and my family," or "I really value focus and am choosing to focus my full attention on my role as a mother for now."

When you openly share your decisions with other people, you are speaking your truth and strengthening your commitment to the mother you want to be.

CHAPTER FIVE

Step 5
SETTING YOUR INTENTION

*"Be who you are and say what you feel, because those who mind
don't matter and those who matter don't mind."*
—Dr. Seuss

Babies come with the purest intentions. Even when they sit with oatmeal dripping from their hair, they seem so innocent. No matter how mad you get at them when they've interrupted your phone call for the fifth time or spit up on your cashmere sweater, you can forgive them almost anything with a glance from those big baby eyes. Instantly, you swing from irritation to adoration, as once again you're filled with love.

In this chapter, we teach you how to do this *for yourself.* You will learn how to shift your thinking away from negative self-defeating or counterproductive thoughts and replace them with a mindset more aligned with your values. You do this by setting your intention.

A State of Being

Your intention is a concise statement summarizing the state of mind that you choose as your approach to life. Your intention helps you stay mindful of who you *intend* to be, even in the midst of the changes and challenges of new motherhood. It starts with "I am" and ends with the way you want to be. Here are some examples:

"I am loving, playful, and relaxed."

"I am a happy, adaptable person who does her best."

"I am bold and irreverent!"

"I am a beginner who is eager to learn something new."

"I am grateful."

Each of these intentions describes a mindset you could hold at any given moment.

At first glance, intentions may look like beliefs or goals. But intentions have some specific characteristics. An intention is not a goal that you achieve such as "I want to get through labor with no medication," nor is it an action that you take like "I commit to keeping my baby's scrapbook up to date." Rather, it is a condition you want to embody such as "I am focused and committed." You might or might not *believe* that you are focused and committed at any given moment, but it's how you *want* to be. Unlike goals and actions that take some time to attain, your intention works instantaneously. An intention has momentum and helps to pull you forward into a specific state of being.

Here's an example. Imagine yourself with a 3-week-old baby. It's six o'clock in the evening. The washer is stacked with burp cloths, the diaper pail is overflowing, your sweatshirt smells like spit-up, and your husband's late from work. You feel frustrated, tired, and doubtful about whether you can make it through another wakeful night. Inwardly you feel out of balance; outside, you are irritable and abrupt. It could be very difficult to pull yourself out of that negativity until you remember your intention: "I am loving, playful, and relaxed." Suddenly you feel a shift, realizing that there is a different way to approach this very moment. There, in the middle of the chaos, is the sweetest baby face you've ever seen. You do relax, you connect to the love you feel, and you start to play with your baby's teeny toes. The laundry can wait. Your intention gives you something to hold on to. It has the power to change your perspective, open your mind, and shift your experience.

> *"I am one passionate and bulldog mama!"*   —LISA, **9** MONTHS PREGNANT

Later in this chapter, you will create a single intention to define how you want to be as a mother. This intention, along with your values and beliefs, will help you keep your balance when life with a baby gets rocky. Your intention can be used for any situation from birthing pains to busy days. You can use your intention throughout pregnancy and motherhood.

> *"My big realization was that I could use an intention now, while I am still pregnant. I have started to say 'I am a remarkable human being with a miraculous body' every time I get cranky about my back pain and exhaustion!"*   —MELISSA, **6** MONTHS PREGNANT

Remembering You Have a Choice

Intentions bring you back when you wander away from who you want to be. Unlike journaling, meditating, counseling, and deep conversation, which are also great ways to find yourself when you're feeling lost, your intention is 100 percent available no matter where you are or what you're doing. You don't have to wait until the time is right to connect with your intention. It can help you in the middle of the night, driving in the car, or in line at the grocery store. It doesn't take any special skill or knowledge—only the awareness that you're not feeling like yourself and a commitment to redirect your thoughts.

Understandably, you might not always be able to be the woman you intend to be. Sometimes it feels good to be grumpy. But when you're feeling the wear and tear of a challenging day, an intention can be the shot of inspiration you need. Just having an intention reminds you that you have a choice about how to experience everything that's happening in your life. The right intention can compel you to change your point of view in the moment and become—again and again—the kind of mother you intend to be.

> *"On those crazy days where I start questioning myself as a mother, I repeat my intention to myself, as a kind of mantra. It helps snap me out of my self-defeating garbage-talk."*   —SUSAN, MOTHER OF ONE

FINDING YOUR OWN WAY
Setting Your Intention

You now create an intention that embodies who you intend to be in the first year of motherhood—a single statement to keep you centered and focused throughout the ups and downs of your new life.
You will have the chance to experiment with different ways of being until you find what most inspires you. If you want more help, we include further instructions in "A Closer Look." Your intention, along with your values and beliefs, completes your "Foundation for Motherhood" in the "Keepsakes" section in the back of the book.

How you set your intention matters. Intentions are most effective when they are simple, positive, and phrased in the present tense as if the statement is already happening. Using the form "I am . . ." instead of "I will . . ." or "I want . . ." packs more punch. Notice the difference between "I want to be patient as a new mother" and "I *am* patient as a new mother."

To create your intention, start by asking yourself the following questions:

- ❷ Who do I want to *be* in the first year of motherhood?
- ❷ *How* do I want to experience my life?
- ❷ What *mindset* or *perspective* do I want to hold?

What adjectives come to mind? Go ahead and jot them down. Try putting the words together in a sentence that expresses your intention as a sample.

Imagine using your sample intention in different situations after the baby is born. For example, Joyce picked "I am adventurous" for her intention. She thought about what "I am adventurous" would be like in labor, during midnight feedings, spending time with her husband, and in balancing her life and her career. Suddenly Joyce's outlook on life with a new baby was infused with spirited enthusiasm, as she imagined how every aspect of her life could become part of the adventure.

See what changes for you as you apply your intention to the different areas of your life. Do it now. Say your intention aloud and add different endings: "at work," "at home," "with my friends," "with my husband/partner," or "in my community." What do you notice? How does your intention influence each area of your life?

Setting your intention is an opportunity for creativity. Play with different intentions, trying them on for size. What would it be like to be fearless in your approach to new motherhood? Organized? Whimsical? Conscientious? Trusting? Adept? Each intention offers you new possibilities.

You may find many options—so many that you are tempted to use them all in one giant intention stuffed with descriptive words. Instead, relax and experiment. It should feel more like choosing an ice cream flavor than packing a suitcase; you get to taste many flavors, then choose *one* that appeals to you now. In the end you need to create a single intention that you will easily remember and keeps you focused on who you want to be. For more suggestions, see "A Closer Look."

Be sure to use your intention right away! Place your intention where you will see it regularly. Type it up in a striking font. Write it on a banner with colorful markers. One expecting mother made a laminated card with her intention and put it in the diaper bag. Don't forget to share your intention with your husband or partner.

KEEPSAKE

Write down your intention in "My Foundation for Motherhood" in the "Keepsakes" section in Appendix A or in your own journal or notebook.

TIPS FOR SETTING YOUR INTENTION

- Make your intention clear and concise.
- Phrase your intention in the present tense.
- Use compelling adjectives. Try lots on for size.
- Place your intention where you can see it.
- Memorize it! Use it!

Common Experiences

Setting intentions can be such a rich experience. It's like trying on colored glasses; every new intention makes the world appear a little different. Even more exciting, you get to choose the way you will look at the world from now on. This process affects women in various ways. Here are some other expectant mothers' experiences.

Doing It Your Own Way. Many women break the rules of intentions to find the words that really work for them. Molly was one mother who needed to do it her own way. "I ended up with a long intention but quite frankly, it represents me best. When I say it, I feel like I'm ten feet tall! Here it is: 'I am an authentic, confident, creative, connected, entitled, flexible, patient, present, and trusted woman.'" Even though a more succinct intention would be easier to learn by heart, this one contained everything Molly most wanted to remember.

Some mothers like to use metaphors in their intentions. A few months before her baby was born, Nancy exclaimed, "I love new experiences. I want to be able to just jump off the springboard and see what it's like! To look at this as a totally new experience." Her intention, "I am jumping off the springboard!" might not mean much to anyone else, but for Nancy, it helped retain the sense of glee that she wanted to define her as a mother.

Other mothers have used seemingly negative ideas to create very powerful intentions. Mina set the intention to be "irresponsible" ("*Finally* I don't have to be the one who has to keep it all together!"). Lucy also felt liberated when she set her intention to be "good enough" ("It feels so good to not have to do everything perfectly.") Both of these women became more forgiving of themselves when they let go of unrealistic expectations of who they were supposed to be and instead chose intentions that allowed them to be themselves.

Whether your intentions are extra long like Molly's, metaphorical like Nancy's, or some other entirely new approach you make up, the important thing is that they work for you.

Counteracting Doubt and Fear. Some women find that the simple act of choosing an intention chases doubts and fears away. Jen was concerned about doing things right. There was so much to learn about having a baby! What if she didn't hold him correctly, couldn't make him stop crying, or wasn't able to bathe him in that tiny tub? Just thinking about it made her heart race.

Setting an intention helped Jen regain a sense of balance. She said, "I'm trying to create the mindset that it's okay. I'm going to make mistakes, but I'll be fine. So what if I don't quite wash the belly button correctly or whatever, the baby's probably fine! I don't even know where I'm going to mess up, but I'm trying to give myself permission to do that. I'm allowing myself to be a first-timer." Suddenly the goofs she might make in mothering seemed rather harmless, and instead of fear, she felt amused by the naïve errors she might make. An intention for Jen to be "an enthusiastic first-time mother" would help her make this shift again and again as each day brought new learning. As it did for Jen, an intention has the power to replace doubt and fear with conscious choice.

Making Changes Now. The immediacy of intentions makes them so attainable that some women start making changes right away. Layla set the intention to be more "conscious"—something she hoped would move her from her typical multitasking manner into a way of being more present when her baby arrived. Using her intention that same day, Layla started noticing different things about her life that she wanted to change now before the birth.

For instance, Layla became aware that ever since she and her husband got married, they had been sitting on the floor at a coffee table watching TV during dinner. To her, it hardly seemed a "conscious" way of eating, neither one of them paying much attention to the food, the experience, or each other. Moreover, it didn't fit at all with her image of wanting to eat together as a family once her baby was born. That day, she stepped out of her habit and into her intention. And that evening, she and her husband sat down to dinner at the dining room table! You don't have to wait to live the life you want. Go ahead and start right now.

Impacting Your Whole Worldview. Many women have been surprised to see the potential for their intentions when they applied them to their entire lives. For instance, Maggie described herself as "intense" and "focused." "When I start a project, I want to finish it!" She worried how she would fare with a spontaneous, unpredictable baby. In the process of trying out intentions, she hit upon this: "I am easygoing as a new mother." She giggled, "That would be a switch!" In that moment, she glimpsed a whole new way of life. What if she became easy-going not just as a new mother but as a businesswoman, a friend, and a wife? The realization that you can choose your experience *in every area of your life* can be startling and impact your life in a big way.

Getting into It. Once you get the hang of setting intentions, you may really get into it! We are encouraging you to set *one* memorable intention for your life as a new mother, but this tool is flexible and easy enough to use in a number of ways. You may intend to be "diligent" about safety and "footloose" about playing with your baby, "forthcoming with emotions" with your husband or partner and "private and reserved" at work. From the way you choose friendships to the way you tackle chores, your intention helps you choose the way you want to be.

The Best of Intentions

Becoming a Mother is about creating life as you intend it to be.

You have stated who you want to be as a mother. You have also learned a skill that will help you move away from thoughts and feelings that drag you down and into those that raise you up—right there and then, in the moment.

As with so many exercises in this book, setting your intention is one that you don't have to wait to try out. Choose any area of your life—right now! today!—that you would like to take on. Try using your intention and see how it changes your experience.

By purposefully choosing who you want to be, you enter motherhood with the best of intentions.

Who do I *really* want to be?

C O N G R A T U L A T I O N S !

You have completed your intention for motherhood! We want to acknowledge you for
- Exploring who you want to be.
- Allowing yourself to experiment with different possibilities.
- Setting your intention.
- Choosing your approach to life.

A Closer Look

Exercise: Playing with Intentions

The more intentions you try, the more expansive your awareness will become! There are so many different ways to be as a mother. Below we give you the chance to go back to the drawing board and keep trying on intentions, then help you test them out and claim the one that speaks to you most.

- **Trying on more intentions.** While setting your intention, it helps to get out of your own box and explore a new way of being. Just for fun, play with some ideas about how you could be in your new way of life! What would the first year of motherhood be like if you were…

creative	light	sassy
fearless	curious	thoughtful
loose	sparkly	intense
wild	powerful	eager
structured	humorous	fluid
tender	passionate	strong
generous	authentic	intuitive
vulnerable	tranquil	sensitive
streamlined	goofy	patient

Go ahead, think of some more adjectives. Try different combinations such as "I am fearless, patient, and sassy." Which words or combinations make you smile? Call to you? Put you off? Which way would *you* like to live?

EXTRA RESOURCES

Remember that we have an electronic version of your "Foundation for Motherhood" worksheet at **www.empoweredmotherhood.com** so that you can keep your values, beliefs, and intention out where you can see them everyday.

Only you can decide who you want to be and how you want to experience life, but you can also expand the intention to include others. How do you want to be as a family, and how does that help clarify your choice? How does your husband or partner want to be? What might your baby want?! What influence does that have on your intention?

- **Testing your intention.** Choose one intention to experiment with. See how it fits with the realities of having a baby. What would it be like to live this intention right now, on this very day? During the rest of the pregnancy? During labor? In the first few days of having the baby home with you? With your husband or partner? On a daily basis with your baby? At work? With friends? With other mothers? Keep trying this thought experiment with different intentions until you find the one that feels right.

- **Claiming your intention.** Finally, having explored all your options, ask yourself one more time, "Who do I want to be as a woman and mother?" Write down your intention.

Find a way to make it concrete. Pick something that symbolizes your intention—a picture, an object, even a piece of jewelry, or at the very least, your piece of paper as a reminder of who you want to be.

Be sure to add your intention to "My Foundation for Motherhood" in the "Keepsakes" section in Appendix A.

Lessons in BECOMING A MOTHER

Lesson 5 Remembering What's Most Important

Honor your true priorities.

Having a baby is no small feat! You will undertake an enormous amount of preparation getting ready for labor and delivery, bringing the baby home, and learning to care for a new little being. The months that follow can be equally busy! There is so much to think about and remember. Keeping your values, beliefs, and intention alive during this time will ensure that you're connected with your best ideas about who you are or who you want to become.

Concrete reminders are one way to do that. We call them your *cues*.

Cues are tangible reminders that jog your memory about what's important to you in the midst of a bustling life. Here are some examples.

- Kate hung an ornament of a smiling black bear near her kitchen window to remind her of her intention to be "gentle and cuddly" with the people she loves and "fierce" with anyone who threatens them.

- Letty put a hand-painted plate given to her by two close friends on her shelf to remind her of the value of friendship.

- Mary wore a crystal bracelet to remind her of her belief that "mothers are as precious as babies."

- Kari kept her daughter's starfish rattle in her purse to remind her of the intention to be "playful."

- Cindy posted a greeting card of a little boy and girl holding hands on her desk to cue her belief that "people come first."

- Jeannie wrote her list of values on a piece of stationery and tacked it up on the wall.

- Sarah changed her email password to "freedom" to remind her every day of her intention to be "free from guilt, fear, and doubt."

- Mel scrawled her core beliefs on a notepad that she kept in the console of her car.

Cues run the gamut from simple to creative. They don't need to be elaborate, and they may not make sense to anyone but you. All that matters is when you see them, they literally remind you of who you are.

To find a cue, ask yourself what kind of object could represent your value, belief, or intention. You're looking for a symbol. You might take an object that you already have and ascribe meaning to it. Or you might go out looking for a new object to serve as your reminder. Either way works.

Cues bring what is most important into your everyday life. Without them, your values, beliefs, and intention can easily be forgotten—just another exercise you once did while reading a book. But they're worth so much more. Bring your brilliant ideas into the physical world where they can remind you of who you are and who you want to be.

CHAPTER SIX

Step 6
DECIDING WHAT YOU WANT

"Keep only those things you love."
—Sara Ban Breathnach

As you get closer to your baby's arrival, chances are that you've started making lists—shopping lists, to do lists, lists of names. You may already have registered at the baby store for everything from bottles to bibs. But as you now know, what you want for yourself is just as important as what you want for your baby. In this chapter, you get to decide what you want as a new mother. Instead of registering for your baby gifts, it's like registering for your life.

But, this time you are not just registering for *stuff*. You'll be deciding on less tangible (but equally important) items, like the emotions you want to surround your life, the arrangements that will make your new life possible, and agreements with other people to make your ideas a reality.

Creating a concrete list of what you want for your new life as a mother is a move from what's *possible* to what *will be*. You are leaving dreaming behind and declaring what you intend to have. Just as sure as you will bring that baby into the world, you are making your new life happen.

Knowing Exactly What You Want

In this chapter, you decide *exactly* what you want for your new life. You will make a prioritized list of what you need to create the life that reflects your values, beliefs, and intention. You practice answering the question, "What do I want?" in a way that honors who you really are while also taking reality into account.

This list is not a to do list of things you need to finish before the baby comes. You'll tackle that later, when you make an action plan for your new life. Nor is this a dreamy wish list, for these are things that you actually intend to obtain. Instead, the list you are making now is most like a shopping list—a collection of defined, concrete details describing what you want in your new life.

Your list will contain your specific desires for new motherhood. It can be a combination of the practical (like a great jog stroller), the abstract (like peace of mind), the mundane (diapers stacked at the ready), the exhilarating (confidence in a new phase of life), the public (a day to introduce your baby to your co-workers), and the private (a purse-sized photo album just for you). You determine which things will make the biggest difference in helping you feel fulfilled as a woman and a mother. Ultimately, as you focus your energy, you take action, and make the necessary changes in your life, your list will be your guide.

Right now you don't have to worry about *how* you're going to make your list happen. You will do that in coming chapters. Although you are moving closer to reality, don't allow it to cramp your imagination. This is your chance to declare what you seriously want in your life and what you intend to create.

The Art of Prioritizing

What would it be like to keep only those things you love? What would you have in your life? What things might fall away? After creating the list of what you want for your new life, you will put it in order.

This kind of prioritizing goes beyond the divide-and-conquer approach you might use for a daily chores list. Instead, you will identify what's *most important* above all else. You will decide what's essential versus what's important or merely nice to have. What you end up with is not just a list, but a deep and meaningful sense of what your life will be about.

The art of prioritizing requires focus and discernment, as well as a sense of connection to what matters most to you. All of the thinking and work you have done so far plays into this process and leads you to this moment. Let prioritizing be a crystallizing moment, where it all comes together: your wants, your reality, your values, beliefs, and intention—captured in a concrete, attainable vision for your life.

> *"I'm so used to just trying to get everything done on my task list and often putting my husband and friends on the bottom of the list. I don't want to do that with my baby. I don't want to do that in my life any more. Prioritizing tasks based on my values is a pretty radical and necessary leap for me."* —ANITA, 6 MONTHS PREGNANT

Setting Your Life in Motion

Before you make your list, know that by deciding that you really want something—*decide*, not just think about—you automatically set the wheels in motion. Deciding starts the change process and focuses your efforts.

Deciding what you want rests on an important reality: *You get to choose how you want your life to be.* It seems obvious, but it can be easy to forget. Many women, not just mothers, fall into the trap of thinking that "this is just the way my life *is*." It's absolutely vital that you realize you are living by choice at any moment in your life.

Creating your prioritized list is your opportunity to affirm what you value and what you want to keep in your life, what you want to add, and what no longer fits. At a minimum, you have the power to choose your reactions, your attitude, who and what you surround yourself with, and where you put your energy.

Even if you change your mind later, deciding what you want now is a valuable exercise. You are not creating a locked-down plan that you can't deviate from. You are being purposeful about going after what you *do* want at this moment. It's also about having a reminder and a touchstone so you don't lose yourself when life *does* change. Declaring what you want at any given time is an invaluable skill—one that will keep you light on your feet throughout the changes of new motherhood and the rest of your life.

FINDING YOUR OWN WAY
Making Your List

Now you are going to claim what you really want for your new life as woman and mother by creating your own prioritized list. You can do this by yourself, with your husband or partner, or you both can create lists separately and compare notes afterwards. Make a short list to play with in this chapter or sit down and add all the details. The more complete your list is, the closer you are to creating the life you want. In "A Closer Look" we offer additional questions to assist you in finishing your list.

Go over everything you have learned so far in reading this book. Take a look at the notes from your exploration and vision for your ideal first year. Review your thinking around the values, beliefs, and intention you chose. Let it all settle in your mind.

Now, with no hedging, no worrying, and no kidding: What do you *really* want? Get out your pen and paper and develop your list! Imagine yourself filling out that life registry—putting down everything you would really like to have in your life (being realistic and optimistic at once), not knowing whether you'll ever actually get it. Declare what will fulfill your vision for your first year of motherhood. What you desire may range from a diaper service to a work-from-home business, from a good massage to a renewed relationship with your husband or partner, from a smarter budget to a part-time nanny. Remember, there are no judgments about what you "should" want, just encouragement to list what makes sense to you.

You are entitled and empowered to state what you *really* want—even if you are still not sure how to get it. If you are hesitating, try asking yourself: "If I knew I could have what I wanted, would I ask for this?" If the answer is yes, write that item down! Your honesty might lead to a solution in the coming chapters. However, if you hold back in your list, you may prevent the chance for the inspired, clever, or serendipitous solutions to emerge.

Make sure that you are clear on exactly what you want. Maybe you dreamed big when you first started this process and imagined a new house on a cul-de-sac with a huge yard, friendly neighbors, and an adorable puppy. Now, you decide how serious you are about that vision. Maybe you really do want a new house and are ready to consider moving before the baby is born. Or maybe all you want is to clean up and organize your current home so it feels more spacious.

You may be able to list what you want off the top of your head, or you may need time to reflect. Try these questions now to generate additional items for your list.

❷ What else will help me live according to my values, beliefs, and intention?

❷ Does my list address all aspects of my life? For example, home, career, relationships, and personal growth?

❷ If I do/have/become all of these things, will I be living the life I want?

There is no perfect size for your list—some women have five items, some have fifty. What does matter is that each item is a "what" not a "how." This is not a list of the actions to get what you want. It is not a task list of what to finish before the baby comes. It is a list of *what* you want in the first year. For example, you *would* include "yoga and aerobics" or "part-time babysitter" or "a closer relationship with my sister." You *would not* include "call the yoga studio" or "ask other mothers for names of babysitters" or "schedule time with Janet."

Put in the effort to write down what you truly desire. Remember there is extra help in "A Closer Look."

FINDING YOUR OWN WAY
Prioritizing Your List

The next step is to prioritize so that you know where to focus your energy for the biggest results. One effective method is to organize your list according to the following categories:

- **Catalysts** would create the life you envision if you did or had nothing else.
- **Important Items** will genuinely influence your ability to be the kind of woman and mother you wish to be.
- **Nice-to-Haves** are not absolutely necessary.
- **Items to Let Go** have to be out of the way so your ideal first year can emerge.

Organizing your list this way keeps you focused on what's most important.

Evaluate your list. What catalysts do you see? Be careful to avoid the trap of feeling like everything is a number one priority. Ask yourself these questions to help you sift through your list and find the catalysts.

❓ What is essential to my happiness and fulfillment as a new mother?

❓ What one thing will do the most to make the first year fall into place?

❓ What items would I regret not having by my baby's first birthday?

Catalysts are different for every woman. Heile's catalyst was "flex time," which she defined as working two days a week from home. She believed that the combination of continued interaction at the office and flexibility at home was the key to the balance she craved. Elaine's catalyst was "having my mother stay with us for the first month." Elaine felt that convincing her mother take an extended trip would make everything else work—uninterrupted sleep, nurturing meals, and moral support—all resulting in time for Elaine to find her way as a new mother.

Now circle those items that you feel are your catalysts. Be bold enough to claim them. These are the choices that will create the life you want. Even if you still do not know how to make them happen, it's enough for now to know you want them!

Once you've established your catalysts, prioritizing the rest of your list is a downhill ride. Go ahead and identify the next tier of items—what's important to remember and create for your life, but not vital. Ask yourself: Which of the items on this list will genuinely influence my ability to be the kind of mother I want to be? Note the items that fit.

What's left on your list? These are your nice-to-haves! For many women, the process of prioritizing shows that there are some things that aren't that important. That's good. Just because you could have something in your life doesn't mean you have to. Some things, no matter how pleasant they might be, simply don't justify the time or attention they require.

On the other hand, you never know what circumstances might make the nice-to-haves possible, so you don't have to throw them out. Notice that these remaining items are less important and allow them to be optional in your life. Release any pressure about *having* to have them.

If you want extra help prioritizing your list, "A Closer Look" has suggestions for a more thorough approach.

TIPS FOR CREATING YOUR PRIORITIZED LIST

- Don't list tasks—list *what you want* for your first year.
- Include items for all areas of your life.
- Try limiting your catalyst items to no more than five.
- Be sure to collaborate with your partner!

KEEPSAKE

Copy all your work to "My Prioritized List" at the end of the book or into your own journal or notebook.

FINDING YOUR OWN WAY
Letting Go

One final step before you stop prioritizing. Now that you have clearly laid out what you want, it's time to be honest about what you don't want—or at least what you can live without. Look closely at your life and inside yourself to realize what you need to let go of. Having the life you want isn't just about putting things into your life; it's also about moving things out of the way.

Ask yourself the following questions and write down your immediate thoughts with no second-guessing:

❓ Where am I spending time currently that doesn't fit with my priorities?

❓ Who am I making time for now that isn't really important to me after all?

❓ What activities am I engaged in that don't match my values or beliefs?

❓ What kinds of tasks do I dislike to do and don't actually enhance my life?

Letting go isn't always easy—especially when you see some things that used to be near and dear to you on that list. It also can be challenging to let go of old issues and habits. As one mother-to-be said, "This might be the hardest part of the process. Even things I absolutely want to let go of, like guilt or self-doubt, have that familiarity and odd comfort quality to them." Have the courage to write down what you truly wish to let go. Give up the "good" for the "best." When your baby arrives, you will have the space and freedom your family needs.

KEEPSAKE

Copy all your work to "My Prioritized List" in the "Keepsakes" section in Appendix A or in your own journal or notebook.

EXPECTANT MOTHERS LET GO!

"I let go of obligations."   —BELINDA

"I'm letting go of my volunteer work . . . for now. Maybe after the baby is born, I'll want to pick it back up, but right now it's stressing me out to think of how I'll fit it all in. So I'm letting it go."   —SAVANNA

"I'm letting go of needing the baby's room to be like a perfect magazine picture."
—Daniela

"I'm letting go of the unimportant."   —JOAN

"I let go of excessively questioning myself and my ability to be a good mother. I'm letting go of the need to be perfect."   —PAIGE

"I'm letting go of my so-so friendships. It's hard to call them that, but honestly, some friendships have become almost a duty. They take up time I want to spend getting ready for the baby, it's time to let them go."   —MAE

"I'm letting go of THINGS. I let go of thinking that the best baby gear will make me a better mother."   —GRACE

"I'm letting go of my intense workouts. I'm also going to let go any expectations of how long it will take to get my body 'back to normal.'"   —JEN

Common Experiences _____

Declaring what you want is a truly significant step. It can be challenging as well as empowering. Here are some of the things you might find as you go through this process.

Coming Up Blank. Many women struggle to say what they want because they know it might change. As Becky put it, "You never know how you're going to feel after your baby is born." Even if you don't know everything you'll want as a new mother, your list gives you a place to start. For example, one woman didn't know whether she would want to work at her current job after the baby was born, but she *did* know that she wanted to be balanced, feel stimulated, and earn a certain amount of money. On her list, she simply wrote these three items:

- Balance
- Stimulation
- Enough money to cover our expenses (with a little bit of a "cushion" left over)

So much about being a new mother involves the unknown. Focusing on what you *do* know brings you back to familiar territory.

Second-Guessing Yourself. Sometimes simply asking the question, "What do I want?" is a leap. There are so many other ways to decide what to do in life—by doing what *has* to be done, what everyone else is doing, what you think you *should* do, or what someone else wants you to do. It can be jarring, if exhilarating, to realize that you can simply say what you want!

Maya was one mother who second-guessed herself. She hesitated to admit that she wanted time to go to yoga every morning. She felt selfish asking for this, it seemed like too much time for herself. She had assumed she would have to give up yoga after the baby arrived. She could hear the objections of her husband if she actually suggested leaving him alone with the baby when he was supposed to be getting ready for work. She started to brainstorm how she might be able to make it happen. Maybe she could just meditate at home or buy a yoga tape. Maya started rationalizing that maybe she could give up yoga for the first year; then she started rationalizing why she *had* to practice yoga in the first year. In a matter of moments, she was tangled in a web of assumptions, vacillation, possibilities, questions, and confusion.

She had to stop her mind from spinning. Maya asked herself again, "What do I *want?*" The answer came: "I want time for myself, and I want yoga." That's what she wrote on her list.

Wanting a New Way of Life. You may discover that what you want goes way beyond what you expected. Ava's biggest ah-ha moment happened when she saw that her identity was expanding. "Before now, my theory at work has always been that if somebody needed to stay up all night and draft something, then I was willing to do it. My work was my priority. Now, I can see that it's not going to be the same after the baby. But it will be really hard to not be little Miss Johnny-on-the-Spot. It's going to be hard for me to say no. But I know that if I don't, I'll be kicking myself, because I hate, hate, hate the idea of spending any less time with my daughter than I want to." Wanting to capture this feeling in her list, Ava wrote, "making my family my priority."

Ava's experience illustrates an important point. When you start to get specific about what you want, you may find that big changes lie ahead. In addition to what you want for your baby, you just might want a new way of life.

Asking from the Heart. Your "life registry" can lead to self-discovery. In her reflection about what she wanted, Dianna asked herself what would help her stay true to herself as a new mother. The answer surprised her. It wasn't even one of the things she had marked as important so far on her list. It was *self-permission*. Dianna realized that she hadn't been giving herself permission to let the baby be a priority along with the other things that mattered to her. In her final list, self-permission was her number one catalyst. It wasn't concrete and it wasn't tangible, but Dianna knew what it meant. She felt that with self-permission, everything else she wanted would fall into place. The most powerful lists come from the heart, not from any preconceived ideas about what kinds of ideas they "should" contain.

Getting Ideas. The simple act of naming what they wanted has generated creative, inspired ideas from many women who have moved from "that can't happen" to "maybe it can." In the box entitled, "What Women Want," some expectant mothers share a few of the things they most desire for motherhood.

WHAT WOMEN WANT . . .

. . . AT WORK

"I want to continue being a role model for other women with my career."
—WENDY

"I want to stop being a workaholic, where I always think, 'I'll just work a couple more hours, I'll get it done,' and then I feel guilty when I leave."   —CAROL

"I want more focus. Maybe cut back on lunches out...to start working through lunch so I could get home faster to the baby."   —HEATHER

"I want my career to continue just as it is now. I want maternity leave to just be a small little blip. A little break."   —HOLLY

"I would like to be able to work half days every day for five or six hours in the mid-dle of the day. I don't mind working five days a week, I just would like not to be working fourteen hours a day." —LEESHA

. . . FOR TIME OFF

"I want to take two to three weeks off before the baby comes to get really ready and be totally relaxed and rested for him to arrive." —MAYA

"I want to be able to take six months off...but I want it to be flexible. I want to have the option of going back to work earlier if I'm ready." —TRACY

"I want my entire maternity leave to be about my baby." —NANCIE

"I want to be present and connected with my baby." —CAMI

. . . FOR THEIR HUSBANDS AND PARTNERS

"I want my husband to feel comfortable and supported in being a father. He didn't have the best childhood, so it's important to me that he feels involved." —JAN

"I hope that I can come home and cook meals and help out with projects around the house so I don't neglect my partner." —PATTY

"I want for my partner and me to figure out a really good way of communicating and compromise with this added element to our lives." —JENNY

"I want time for my husband to have his own relationship with the baby." —MADISON

. . . FOR THEIR BABIES

"My vision is that I'll be secure in the knowledge that my child is in really good pro-fessional care when he's not with me—a wonderful and educational and creative environment so he's growing and learning." —BOBBI

"I hope that I can teach my daughter everything that I want to teach her and spend the quality time I want to spend with her so she grows up to be a really loving, great, smart, intelligent child." —PAULA

"I want one of those front-pack carriers so I can show my baby the world!" —FRANCA

. . . FOR THEMSELVES

"If I had my way, I'd do something more creative for a living. I've always wanted to own my own business. Maybe a scrapbook store or something. I'd like to work at something I love, even if I don't make the world's greatest money at it. I know I would definitely be happier, and it would be great to raise a child in that kind of environment."   —CONNIE

"I honestly hope for the strength and energy to get through these first couple of years, because I think I'm going to be sleep deprived."   —MEGHAN

"I want to be stable financially."   —GRETCHEN

"I want the baby to be sleeping through the night before I return to work so I'm not exhausted every day."   —JULIA

Registering for Your New Life

Claiming things for yourself isn't always easy. It requires a sense of entitlement that's not always second nature for women. It is your right and your privilege as a mother to create a life that works for you—*all* of you, including your husband or partner, and your baby.

You have defined the details that will add up to the life you want. You have chosen the catalysts, those things that will make the biggest difference in your life. You have identified what you can let go.

Declaring what you want in your life doesn't make it so. That only comes with action, which you'll undertake in the coming chapters. Nor does prioritizing mean you have a clear path ahead. You'll need to address any fears and obstacles that have surfaced, and you will. You have the strength, courage, ability, and the will to create change in your life. It's time to go after what you want!

 An Inquiry for You | What am I claiming?

C O N G R A T U L A T I O N S !

You have really stepped up in this chapter as you created your prioritized list for your new life. We want to acknowledge you for

- Declaring what you want.
- Deciding what's most important above all else.
- Determining what to let go of.
- Moving from what's possible to what will be.

A Closer Look

Below are two exercises to help you finish your prioritized list of what you want when your baby arrives. The first gives you ideas for adding items to your list. The second gives you a detailed approach for prioritizing those items. We also included a sample list from one our mothers at the end.

Exercise 1: Completing Your List

If you want to make the most of your opportunity to design your new life, you'll want your prioritized list to be as thorough as possible. You do that by reviewing your efforts in *Becoming a Mother*, assessing your whole life, and organizing your ideas into a cohesive, functional list.

> • **Reviewing your efforts.** If you haven't already, make sure you have thoroughly reviewed all the work that you have done in this process and capture that thinking in your list. Here are some reminders.

- You explored and answered questions around your thinking about motherhood and about life. Remember any insights that are especially important.

- You imagined a life for yourself as a mother in which everything was just as you would like it to be. Think about the wisdom your vision held for your real life.

- You are more clear about who you are—what's important to you, what you believe, and who you want to be. Read your values, beliefs, and intention out loud and think about what they mean to you.

After revisiting your work, see what new items you can add to your list.

> • **Look across your life.** Are there any areas in your life that you have overlooked? In thinking about your first year, what do you want for your . . .

- Relationship with your husband or partner?
- Friends?

EXTRA RESOURCES

An electronic version of a prioritized list worksheet is available at **www.empoweredmotherhood.com.**

- Family?
- Career?
- Passions?
- Health?
- Wealth?
- Growth?
- Spirit?
- Home?
- Budget?
- Schedule?
- Childcare?
- Support system?

Add any important new items to your list!

- **A little organizing.** When you are sure that your list is complete, take a moment to organize. Go back through the list and group items that go together. Group them in the categories of your life or some other organization that makes sense for you.

As you group ideas, add any that come to mind and cross off any that are redundant or not as appealing as you first thought. See what aligns with your values, beliefs, and intention and what doesn't quite fit. At the end, you will have a complete prioritized list that you can use as you get ready to take action!

Be sure to add your work to "My Prioritized List" in the of the book.

Exercise 2: A Prioritization Technique

As with creating your list, prioritizing can present its own set of challenges. Here is a simple technique to help you be more objective and methodical with your prioritizing. After you finish, you will see what naturally moves to the top of the list and what falls to the bottom.

Start by asking this question. "What choices truly honor my values? What things fit perfectly with my beliefs? What items bring my intention to life?" Put a star next to those items on your list. If you need to add something new, do so.

To continue, ask this next question. "If I had to choose just three items from my whole list—which ones have to be there—what do I need first in order for everything else to follow?" Put a star next to those items. If you already have a star, add another! Then continue with the following questions.

"What activities/items would I feel lost without?" Star those, again allowing some items to be accumulating multiple stars.

"Who are the people that are most important to me?" Star the items on your list that express their importance.

"How will I take care of myself? How will I be supported in doing so?" Once again, star items that address these questions.

"What do I want most of all for my baby? What do I want to be teaching him by the way I live my life? What do I want her to know about me and how will she know it?" Find the items on the list that honor this importance and star them.

"What is the one thing that will help me stay true to myself when everything else gets crazy?" Put a star next to that item.

Count all the stars for each item. Based on what you see, make up your own rules for how many stars are necessary for a "catalyst," "important," "nice to have," and to cause an item to drop off. But remember, this is just an exercise! The stars give you direction; you make the final choice of what your list looks like.

Be sure to add your work to "My Prioritized List" in the "Keepsakes" section in Appendix A.

Sample Prioritized List

Catalysts

- *Self-permission—allowing myself time and space to find my own way as a mother.*
- *Maternity leave—at least three months.*
- *A way to get extra sleep for the first month.*
- *Starting grad school.*
- *A different job for Andrew or some way to stop the weekly business travel.*

Important

- *Positive images, sounds, and energy around the baby.*
- *Room for the baby.*
- *A routine for the baby that works for us.*
- *Learning about my baby (classes, some kind of "baby and mommy" weekend?).*
- *Time alone with Andrew!*
- *Ask our families how they want to be involved with the baby.*
- *Stay connected with friends.*
- *Swimming!*
- *Keep journaling.*
- *Time for Andrew to create his own relationship with the baby.*
- *A reasonable but effective exercise and eating plan after the birth?!*
- *Great babysitters.*

Nice to Have

- *Frontpack.*
- *Jogging stroller.*
- *A journal/travelogue of the first year to save for the baby.*
- *A baby-proofed, baby-ready home.*
- *New friends with babies.*
- *No business email or phone calls for first two months.*
- *Breastfeeding class.*

- *Help with cooking and cleaning if I want it.*
- *Good healthy meals in the freezer, ready to go.*

I Let Go of

- *The negative people in my life.*
- *Trying to read all the newsletters in my inbox—just delete them!*
- *Taking a trip to see Andrew's parents in the first few months.*
- *Feeling like I won't be a good mother.*

Lessons in BECOMING A MOTHER

Lesson 6 **Saying No!**

Say no gracefully with certainty and confidence.

You probably have had many opportunities to practice saying "no" during your pregnancy—when your mother-in-law suggested naming the baby after some distant relative, a friend asked you to lunch when you were fantasizing about a catnap, or your boss asked you to take on an extra project just as you were about to cut back. Some women find it easy to answer with a decisive and cheerful, "no, thank you!" Other women hedge or avoid giving an answer. Some women feel so uncomfortable that they end up saying "yes" when they mean "no."

As you go after what you want and let go of what you don't, the skill of saying "no" becomes indispensable.

Saying Yes

Instead of focusing on how hard it is to say no, focus on what you are saying yes to!

Let's say your best friend, who is also pregnant, calls to persuade you to join her Friday evening prenatal swimming class. You hate to say no. She wants to spend time with you and share the fun of pregnancy. Plus it's great exercise, so maybe you should just agree. But you've really been enjoying your quiet evenings at home, especially in these late weeks of pregnancy when you're feeling a little more tired. Instead of doing something you don't want to do and feeling guilty, you choose something you do want and feel content. You thank your friend for the invitation and say, "I'd love to spend time with you, but I'm enjoying every restful evening I can get. How about if we meet for brunch instead?" You get to keep your quiet evenings, and your friend gets to spend special time with you.

By saying no, you are also saying yes to what you want.

Getting Some Perspective

When it comes to saying no, it's easy to blow the consequences out of proportion. Deciding whether to invite your obnoxious cousin to your baby shower may seem like a colossal issue at the time, but given your weak relationship, does it really make that much of a difference? Asking a key question or two can put things back in perspective.

Ask yourself: "Will I remember this decision a year from now?" If not, stop sweating and do what you want. Say no to inviting your cousin and enjoy the day. Depending on the situation, you might ask yourself, "Will this matter when my baby is a year old, 10 years old, or grown up?" "Will I even remember this decision in five years or at the end of my life?"

Teilan uses this technique with consistent results. Whenever she has the inkling she wants to say no, she skips the explanation and weighs the issue. If it's important to her, she says yes. Otherwise she simply says, "I'd rather not." She doesn't apologize, and she doesn't explain. Surprisingly, her friends find it refreshing!

Save deliberation for the big decisions. You don't have to spend your whole life never getting around to what *you* want. It's your life! You have a right to choose.

Concentrating on Your Integrity

Saying no is the perfect time to rely on your "My Foundation for Motherhood." Your values, beliefs, and intention can give you the courage to say no.

Meg was a family physician who made some hard choices before the birth of her baby. Meg practiced with a group of other doctors. The practice was flourishing and all the doctors wanted Meg to stay. But Meg wanted to work part-time and be more involved with her daughter.

Round and round Meg went, struggling to make the right choice. She desperately wanted to say "yes" to an easier life, but she wrestled with the meaning of her leaving. "After all those years in school, am I really going to throw it all away? What kind of message does that send to my daughter? Plus, what impact will my leaving have on the practice?" Perhaps hardest of all, Meg felt almost sick when she thought of turning her back on the business she had helped build. In some ways it was her first "baby" and she really didn't want to let it go.

Meg opened up her "My Foundation for Motherhood." There in black and white were the values of "a quiet heart" and "family first." Her intention read, "I am comfortable and calm." Her chest swelled and her eyes filled with tears. She called her office that very day and announced she would be working part-time.

Just because a decision is right for you doesn't mean it's easy. Like Meg, you may find saying "no" painfully hard. Knowing that doing so safeguards your integrity can lighten the load and help you know when it's the right thing to do.

When deciding what you want for your life, it may help to realize that you are *always* choosing. When you said yes to a baby, you said no to a life on your own. When you said no to living by chance, you said yes to living by choice. Your whole life is made up of your choices. Even when your choice is no, you can choose it with strength and conviction—not apologetically, but joyfully with conviction and grace.

Step 7
MODELING YOUR TIME, MONEY, AND SPACE

"The big secret in life is that there is no big secret. Whatever your goal, you can get there if you are willing to work."
—*Oprah Winfrey*

When your baby joins your family, you will often wonder how such a small person can come with so much *gear*. In every area of your life—your floor space, your bank account, your kitchen table, your closets, your car, you name it—you will have to make room for this baby.

This chapter shows you ways to actually "try on" your life with a baby, to make sure everything will fit. You'll do this by making models for the different areas of your life: areas like your time, your money, and your space. This gives you the chance to see how things fit and where they don't, so that you can identify important questions you might have and find the obstacles in your way.

This is your reality check. You still get to say what you want. But, you also get to see how everything you want might actually work. Get ready: You are about to test out your new life.

Making Models

In this chapter, you will create *models* for the different areas of your life. In modeling, you mock up your ideas from your prioritized list to see how they might actually play out in real life. Just as a sculptor makes a clay model of a vision before chipping away at the stone, you are going to do some trial runs of your ideas before you actually make any life changes.

For instance, you may get out your calendar and try out a few sample schedules. You might crunch some numbers or rework your budget. Perhaps you'll draw some diagrams of areas within your home to show how you'll rearrange space. The idea is to get a sense of how life with your baby *might* look in detail while there's still plenty of time to make changes, plan ahead, and discuss your ideas with the important people in your life.

Models for time might include sample calendars with items from your prioritized list showing up as daily, weekly, or monthly events. A sample week might outline the flexible work-from-home arrangement you listed as a catalyst, showing the days and hours you want to propose to your boss on a blank weekly calendar. A few sample daily schedules might contain different options showing how you and your husband or partner can steal time alone every day—something you designated as important on your prioritized list. A sample year might flag some of those nice-to-haves—maybe a vacation for your wedding anniversary and a deadline by which you'd like to take a four-generation photograph. In this way, your models help you draft the life you want.

It's not just your time that needs modeling; it could be almost any aspect of your life. Maybe it's money. Perhaps your prioritized list included a cloth diaper service or extra help around the house for the first few months. Here your model might be a budget showing cost estimates or a few price comparisons. You can also model space. Let's say you wrote that you want an enclosed backyard for your baby to play in. Your model might be a drawing of the yard or a diagram showing where the fence would go, the swing set, the sandbox, and the garden.

Modeling is a dynamic way to translate your list of "what I want" into "here's what it might look like." Take advantage of the opportunity to play with reality.

A Place for Obstacles

Modeling your life in this way can bring up nagging questions, usually starting with "how?" and "but what about. . . ?" and "what if?" Suddenly as you see what it might take to put your dreams into place, you are confronted with challenges that threaten your success. You need a place to put these challenges so that you can keep moving forward with the knowledge that you will address each issue later. We call this place your parking lot.

Your parking lot is a separate sheet of paper on which to list any issues that arise from your modeling. It can hold all the different things that make you stumble or feel stuck. You might have questions like, "How much does formula cost, and how much will we need?" Perhaps you bump into obstacles, like the fact that your business partner is planning a sabbatical at the same time you're supposed to have your baby. Or you might slam up against some things that just seem impossible, like quitting your job. All of these end up on your parking lot. Review the sample in "A Closer Look" to get an idea of how your parking lot might look.

You are now free to lay out your plans with a calm and trusting attitude. When you hit a bump like realizing you don't have enough money for that kid-friendly car on your list, you can just say, "Hmmm. Looks like we're short on cash!" You scribble "money for new car" as an obstacle on your parking lot and go right ahead with picking a date for buying the new car. No panic, no guilt, no premature decision that you can't have what you want.

A parking lot helps to keep you in a possibility mindset while you create the models for your life. Later, it will help you remove the obstacles in your way.

> *"I am loving the idea of just writing down my roadblocks and dealing with them later! That changes my whole perspective. I tend to obsess about the problem and never get to the solution."* —JINA, 8 MONTHS PREGNANT

A WORD ABOUT PLANNING

Modeling can trigger a little anxiety or procrastination for some women. It is important to know that you are not committing to your sample plans; you are just checking things out! By mapping out models for the things you want *most*, you can determine how close your ideal is to reality.

In this step, you pretend that you can control your life—as if you can plan your schedule, your budget, and your activities exactly how you want and the baby will neatly go along with the plan. Of course that's *probably* not going to happen! Babies come with their own agendas, or *no* agendas but to have what they want and need when they want and need it.

You can't expect your life to turn out exactly as you model it. Life isn't totally predictable (and who would want it to be?). You may find after doing this exercise that you don't want any limits on your schedule, you just want to enjoy life and roll with the punches. That's fine. The purpose of modeling is simply to give you a better idea about what might actually be possible.

The Magic of Modeling

Modeling creates momentum. It puts the world around you on notice that you are serious about what you want! It gets the brain humming and helps you open up to all kinds of solutions, ideas, and resources that could bring you what you need. It provides a framework so you can start to see the next steps on your path and the actions to take.

Modeling also reveals the holes in your plan. For instance, when Kim and Paul sat down to look at their weekly calendar before the baby was born, they had a vague notion that they would "split the childcare tasks fifty-fifty." It wasn't until they saw how this looked on a blank weekly calendar that they realized how complicated it might be. Did fifty-fifty mean Kim would drive the baby to daycare and Paul would pick him up? If so, what would Paul do about his evening partner meetings, and how would Kim's boss react to her getting to work a little late? And that was only about the logistics of daycare; what about feeding, diapering, playgroup, groceries, and bedtime? Who would do what, and when? And what impact was that going to have on their life? The whole exercise was somewhat shocking, yet enormously beneficial. Kim and Paul identified how they could bring this new baby into their lives with as much comfort and as little disruption as possible. Months later, they would look back on this conversation and feel they had dodged a bullet, simply because they had discussed some of the issues in advance!

After creating your models, you will have developed a clearer sense of what life would be like if you were truly living it the way you wanted—the way that's best for you as a woman and a mother.

> *"The level of detail in this process does make approaching the first year feel so much more real. Without this step I couldn't think of breaking it down. It made me start to think about specifics and details. It's valuable because Alex and I have a lot of hopes and wishes, but I think I will be too tired after the baby comes to remember them all. It helps to actually write it down and makes me feel like I have a chance of making it happen."* —LOUISE, 8 MONTHS PREGNANT

FINDING YOUR OWN WAY
Modeling Your Ideal Life

Now you get to try a bit of modeling! You will develop some quick models for time, money, and space as well as start your parking lot. You are translating your wants and needs into practical reality to see what obstacles and questions surface. Your models and parking lot are something concrete to discuss with your husband or partner. If possible, do your modeling *with* your partner—budgets, schedule, and changes to the home are topics for collaboration not conflict. If you need extra guidance, be sure to look in "A Closer Look" for more ideas and the sample parking lot.

As you build models for all the items on your prioritized list, you will end up with a vivid picture of the reality you want to create. It might be a budget that shows how the numbers would work if you had the money you think you need. It might be a schedule that shows you doing all of the activities you do want to do and none of the ones that you don't. It could look like a flowchart, a picture, or a diagram. The result will vary depending on your goals.

Take just a few items from your prioritized list—you can work with your full list later. Use a pen or pencil with a few blank sheets of paper for now. When you are ready, ask yourself, "What would my life look like if I had all these things that I want?"

Modeling Your Time. Begin by creating a model of the first year—the year starting from the baby's birth or maybe a month or so before. Make a simple year calendar on your sheet of paper. Map the items from your prioritized list into the year. Mark significant milestones or decisions. For example, Jillian's catalyst was staying connected to friends, so she picked a month for baby's first road trip to visit old college friends and their new baby. Wanda picked an item around fitness and self-image, so she chose the third month after the baby was due to mark the milestone of restarting her gym membership.

Use the same process to create a few other quick models for an ideal month, week, and day. Figure out how items from your prioritized list fit into these time frames. Do your best to ignore all the unknowns—this is just a pretend schedule. If your catalysts include time alone with your partner but you have no idea who could stay with the baby much less when, just pick a date! One woman arbitrarily designated Saturdays as date night for her ideal week.

You can also work with different blocks of time. One woman modeled an ideal day during the first few weeks at home with the baby and another after she would be back at work. Blythe gave each week in a month a theme, "family/home" (sending pictures to the grandparents, cleaning), "play" (a baby music class, the zoo), "creativity" (cooking, drawing), and "reflection" (napping, journaling). Let your models express your ideal!

Modeling Your Money. Consider your budget. Are there any financial implications for the items on your prioritized list? Create a mini-budget for just a few items to see how the numbers work. Are there costs associated with these items? Savings? Write the numbers down on your piece of paper. If you start to feel some pressure or doubt that some of the things you want are feasible, let those feelings go for now. All you need to do is create the model and note what you need, *not* how to get it today.

You might not have experience creating a budget and modeling your finances. Bonnie decided to use her modeling exercise as an excuse to buy a book on smart money management and to go online for sample household budgets and typical costs associated with having a baby. Seriously delving into her finances was something that Bonnie had meant to tackle for a long time. "What a relief to do this! It's like I am already demonstrating behavior I want my baby daughter to follow someday."

Modeling Your Space. Finally, what about space? Do any of the items trigger the need for changes to the physical space in your home? If so, take a sheet of paper and sketch out the changes that would need to happen to make your item a reality. For instance, one of Linda's catalysts was working from home. The problem was that the only extra bedroom was turning into the nursery, so there was no more space for a home office. For her model, Linda roughed out her idea to move the washer and dryer to the garage and turn the laundry room into a snug little workspace. She also added a few estimated costs to her budget model. Note that you may need to go back and forth between different models as you see what your ideas require.

There is no one perfect way to model. As some women move through the items on their prioritized lists, they go right to the computer and their favorite scheduling software or accounting program. Other women get out their planner or a wall calendar and a calculator. Some just map it out in their head. Whatever techniques you normally use to plan your life will work for modeling now. Most likely you are not new to the process of planning; it's just factoring in your baby that's new. Use all of your familiar tools as you go through this process.

KEEPSAKE

Copy any key components of your work in "My Models" in the "Keepsakes" section in Appendix A or in your own journal or notebook.

TIPS FOR MAKING YOUR MODELS

- Start with just a few items from your list.
- Give yourself plenty of freedom to erase and change your models.
- Keep your notes accessible—add new ideas over time.
- See how your partner's models are similar or different to yours.

FINDING YOUR OWN WAY
Making Your Parking Lot

As you started to play with your time, money, and space, you probably bumped up against a number of issues. Now you can create your parking lot, a place to dump all the potential problems and questions that arise. Review the sample parking lot in "A Closer Look" to see what yours might look like.

Get another piece of blank paper and divide it into three columns: "Questions," "Things That Seem Impossible," and "Obstacles." Revisit the models you created so far and ask yourself these questions:

- ❷ What do I think about my models?
- ❷ How far is my current reality from this ideal?
- ❷ What doesn't seem to fit in my schedule, budget, or home?
- ❷ Where are there conflicts?
- ❷ What are the biggest roadblocks so far? Time? Money? Skills? Information? Attitude?
- ❷ What questions do I have to answer in order to move forward?

Add everything to your parking lot under the three different headings. Create your own headings if necessary!

Many women find it a relief to write down all the nagging questions and concerns they have been carrying since they found out they were expecting a baby. Carla had a bunch of questions around maternity leave policy and politics at her company and was glad to unload them all onto her parking lot. Viviane found that writing down some of her challenges, like "My husband will never be willing to do laundry or clean the toilets," actually made things seem more possible—perhaps her husband would come through if she just asked!

As you list your own thoughts, know that you can simply shelve these quandaries for the moment. Let it free your thinking so that you can keep modeling as if you were confident that all challenges could be resolved. You will work through some of the items on your parking lot in the next chapter.

KEEPSAKE

Copy your final thoughts under "My Parking Lot" in the "Keepsakes" section in Appendix A or in your own journal or notebook.

TIPS FOR MAKING YOUR PARKING LOT

- Include everything that is in your way—large or small.
- There are no stupid questions.
- Keep your parking lot handy as you model. Jot down items as you go.
- Take comfort in having a place to dump all your obstacles and concerns!

Common Experiences

For many women, modeling is truly a reality check. There they are on paper: the blueprints of the life they're creating. It may be the first time they believe their ideas could actually become real. Any number of reactions can occur when you see your plans on the page. Below are some you may experience.

Experiencing a Dawning Awareness. The beauty of a model is you actually get to see what something will look like before you create it. The results can be stunning. Looking at the potential changes in their lives, some women feel terror, elation, or even both at once.

For instance, in modeling her daily routine, high-energy Lily was surprised to discover that her new life might slow her way, way down. Looking over her plan for her first year of motherhood, she noticed that she was creating lots of space, having simple expectations, and predicting a new life rhythm that was slower and calmer. "It's 25 mph instead of 100," she remarked. On the other hand, Carmen was horrified by the prospect of going so slow. "All I will have time to do is feed this child! When will I get anything else done?!"

Regardless of the specific form their modeling takes, many mothers-to-be find the process to be enlightening—an experience that challenges their thinking about what lies ahead.

Moving from Cluelessness to Clarity. As we've mentioned before, being a first-time mother holds a lot of unknowns. For many women, modeling is one process that helps them confront uncertainties in resourceful ways.

Some use their parking lot and turn their "I don't knows" into questions. For one mother, "I don't know whether we'll build onto the house, move, or squeeze in" became "How can we get the extra space we need?"

Other women are immediately energized by what they don't know. At 8 months pregnant, Mary struggled to create a model for her ideal day, saying "I have no clue what my days will look like." At that moment she realized she really didn't know the details about the care and feeding of a newborn. This realization sent her rushing to her bookshelf. "I kind of panicked and started to speed read some of my 'first year' books. Prior to that I was only reading about labor and delivery!"

Finally, some women just work with what they do know. For one woman it sounded like this: "I don't know how much money we're going to need for diapers and formula and everything else. I don't even know how much money we'll have if I decide to cut back on my work schedule. Ok, but what *do* I know? I know that diapers cost at least $15 a pack and that we'll still have my husband's full salary..." and she was off and running again.

Discovering what you don't know is one of the purposes of modeling, as well as an important advantage. Realizing what you don't know spurs you to find out.

Drowning in Details. In modeling your new life, it's possible to start drowning in details. There are so many things to think about at once. For example, Dawn was tempted to do all the planning she possibly could, but soon found it was taking forever! Finally she committed a specific amount of time for each model—she booked a maximum of one hour to play around in her calendar and then she stopped. The next day she spent an hour with her finances and an hour sketching out the baby's room. She reminded herself that she didn't have to plan every moment of her life; she just needed to map out enough ideas to determine next steps. The trick with modeling is to do only enough to get the benefit of the process without getting overwhelmed by everything that lies ahead.

Seeing That It Works, and That It's Worth It. Creating your models can reveal that some things are easier than you think. The one thing you thought was positively impossible may turn out to be a mere decision away. We know one mom who wanted to move two states away to be closer to family—an idea she thought her ladder-climbing career-man of a husband would never go for. It turned out that moving was exactly what he had in mind.

Allie found the process of creating her ideal calendar both rewarding and calming. "I took comfort in seeing each of the parts of myself playing a role in my new life—that I wasn't 'losing' myself. I think it was this during this process that I started to feel at peace with letting go of my away-from-home job. I began to see that I could still get the same satisfaction I get from my job in other activities." Elena is another expecting mother who found that modeling moved her from nervousness to excitement. As she sat looking at her models for the first year, she reported, "Wow. This is literally helping me transition into motherhood."

A Sneak Preview of Your Future

In this chapter, you've taken a significant step—one that many people never take. You've literally designed your new life. You've put pen to paper and become serious about what could be possible, while bravely keeping track of the challenges ahead. By modeling, you have mapped out key areas of your life in order to find how things fit, where they don't, what's missing, and what you still need to create.

Whether you actually live according to these calendars, budgets, and plans is not the point. If you never look at these models again, you will still have taken a huge step: Comparing what you want to what you have, then using that information to make room for your baby. Modeling is somewhat magical—you take your ideas and bring them to life for a moment. It gives you sneak preview of your future. Learning how to model is a skill that you can use for the rest of your life to make any dream come true.

An **Inquiry** for **You**	What am I bringing to life?

C O N G R A T U L A T I O N S !

You have just reached another major milestone by modeling your life. We want to acknowledge you for

- Trying on your new life.
- Identifying obstacles and questions.
- Keeping an open mind.
- Getting closer to making your ideal *real*.

A Closer Look

The most popular areas for modeling focus on time, money, and space. Below we offer a detailed process for each to help you finish your models along with blank worksheets. You will also find a sample parking lot you can use to set up your own.

Exercise 1: Your Ideal Schedule

Time is life. When you model how you will spend your time, you are planning how you will spend your life. Here we give you directions for checking out the effects of new motherhood on your year, months, weeks, and days ahead.

- **Your ideal year.** Start your modeling by taking a broad view of the year ahead. What major milestones will be significant in your year? When will your maternity leave start and end? Are there holidays you want to celebrate a certain way? Are you staying home or traveling? Events you don't want to miss? When do you want to be completely ready for the baby? Maybe you'll note when to start attending a moms' group or book your first massage or haircut. These are all items to include in your model.

You may also want to mark the stages you expect to experience throughout that first year. One stage may last two months, another six. Will you start exercising in phases? Will you be breastfeeding for part of the year or longer? Will there be a phase for getting a routine in place? What would that look like? The idea is to get a sense of the "seasons" ahead—where your emotional state and the practical realities of your schedule will be shifting over the next twelve months.

As you go, use your parking lot. Note anything that seems impossible or is a real obstacle. Jot down any thoughts and questions that surface as you make your calendar for the year.

- **Your ideal month.** Look over your prioritized list again. What is important on a monthly basis? Maybe you want to meet friends for lunch once a month or take

EXTRA RESOURCES

Go to **www.empoweredmotherhood.com** for electronic versions of all the worksheets in this chapter, samples models from real moms-to-be, plus more ideas on how to plan for a new baby.

a day to rest and rejuvenate. Are there some things that could become a monthly ritual to help you live your values, beliefs, and intention? Add them to your plan.

Think about months at different times of the year. What would an ideal month look like for you early in the first year? What about later toward the end? Do all the weeks in a month look the same?

Try a few other months to see what might be different over the year. Look for what stays consistently important month to month. Don't forget to write down questions and obstacles on your parking lot to keep you moving forward.

• **Your ideal week.** Revisit your list again. Where do the things that are most important to you show up weekly? Plot them onto a model for a weekly calendar, filling in activities for each day of the week.

Think about what your ideal week would be at different stages of that first year. One expectant mother looked at when she would return to work full-time. She really thought about how many days she would like to work and which days those would be, as well as the specific hours she would work.

As always, remember to use your parking lot. Natalie wanted to schedule three days a week to sleep in but felt that it could never work with her partner's work schedule. She almost left it out of the plan, but instead penciled it in for two weekdays as well as Sundays. Then Natalie wrote down the question on her parking lot, "How could Michael adjust his schedule to help with the baby two mornings a week?"

• **Your ideal day.** After all this planning, it's time to look at an ideal day. Start with an imaginary day in a specific stage—perhaps a stage you are most concerned about or else one that appeals to you. Consider doing a weekday and a weekend day, or several different kinds of days (such as work days, errand days, days off) if that suits you.

Revisit your list of what you want one more time. See if there are daily items that you can map onto your plan. What are some things you'd like to have happen every day?

• **Your ideal life.** Look at your models together. Run through the following questions to spark additional ideas:

❓ What is my peak time of day, and how do I want to use that time?

❓ What is my low point, and how do I want to use that time?

❓ What one thing brings me the most energy? When will I spend time with that activity?

❓ When do I most want to be with the baby?

❷ What time of the day do I want to keep for myself?

❷ When will my husband or partner have personal time?

❷ When will I have time with friends?

❷ When will I have family time?

❷ What kind of exercise will I get, and when, and how often?

❷ When will I rest?

Be sure to add your work to "My Models" and "My Parking Lot" in the "Keepsakes" section in Appendix A.

Exercise 2: Your Ideal Budget

Review your prioritized list again to determine the financial implications of the things you want. If you keep a budget, get it out and start crunching the numbers. If you don't, jot down a rough budget from scratch.

Play with the numbers to see what it might cost to implement your catalysts versus the items you marked as important versus the nice-to-haves. Some items will have no financial impact—they don't cost you a thing! Other items might not cost anything but do reduce your income, such as working part-time. Still others have obvious or even hidden cost savings. Quitting your job might mean losing that income but enable you to save on commuter costs, lunches out, dry cleaning, and taxes. If you are not sure about the costs for some items, estimate.

Don't forget to check out the budget impact of anything you listed as items you wish to let go. Maybe in your choice to spend more time with your baby, you decide to trade your kickboxing class for long walks in the park. You might decide to let your gym membership go, and with it, the monthly membership fee—which you can now use to pay for other priorities.

What does it all look like? Is this doable? Impossible? Money and budgets are often one of the most stressful topics for new mothers. Jot down all obstacles and questions that pop up during this exercise.

Be sure to add your work to "My Models" and "My Parking Lot" in the "Keepsakes" section in Appendix A.

Exercise 3: Your Ideal Home

Many a mother has marveled at how much space such a small person can take up. See what changes might be required to your home environment for the items on your prioritized list. Ask yourself the following questions:

❷ What new furniture, equipment, and large items do I need to make room for?

❷ What space do I currently have available?

❷ Where could space be freed up?

❷ How could the space change to best support my values, beliefs, and intention?

Start drawing how you would ideally like to use the space you have as well as the space you can create or free up. A corner of the living room might become the special playroom on your prioritized list, helping to honor an underlying value around fun and freedom with your baby.

Expand your thinking to ensure that you are going for your ideal. Often the need to change things for the baby can result in long-desired improvements. For example, a priority item might be childproofing your home. Sketch out how you would really love to make that real. What about clever new lockable cabinets in the laundry room to store away dangerous items *and* all that junk that is cluttering up the room!

As you go through this exercise, record any difficulties on your parking lot.

Be sure to add your work to "My Models" and "My Parking Lot" in the "Keepsakes" section in Appendix A.

<u>*Worksheet*</u>
My Ideal Year

Month:	Month:	Month:
Milestones:	Milestones:	Milestones:
Month:	Month:	Month:
Milestones:	Milestones:	Milestones:
Month:	Month:	Month:
Milestones:	Milestones:	Milestones:
Month:	Month:	Month:
Milestones:	Milestones:	Milestones:

Worksheet
My Ideal Month

Sunday					
Monday					
Tuesday					
Wednesday					
Thursday					
Friday					
Saturday					

Worksheet
My Ideal Week

	Notes
Sunday	
Monday	
Tuesday	
Wednesday	
Thursday	
Friday	
Saturday	

Worksheet
My Ideal Day

6:00 _____

7:00 _____

8:00 _____

9:00 _____

10:00 _____

11:00 _____

12:00 _____

1:00 _____

2:00 _____

3:00 _____

4:00 _____

5:00 _____

6:00 _____

7:00 _____

8:00 _____

9:00 _____

10:00 _____

[add other hours as needed]

Sample "My Parking Lot"

Questions	Things That Seem Impossible	Obstacles
1. What is a likely nap schedule? How much do babies actually sleep? How does it change over the year? 2. Will I actually have enough energy and focus to work with the baby in the house? 3. How much does childcare cost? 4. When is it safe to take the baby out in public? 5. When can I start exercising?	1. Taking three months off. 2. Getting enough sleep 3. Getting enough help. 4. Having enough money to do all of this without going into debt or jeopardizing our future	1. Money. There isn't enough income if I only work three days a week. Plus having childcare and general baby supplies will require more money, not less! 2. Commitments. I don't think I can be as involved in the groups that I have on my plate. 3. Time. There doesn't seem to be enough time to research everything before the baby is born. 4. Room. Currently there is no bedroom for this baby!

Lessons in BECOMING A MOTHER

Lesson 7 **Fighting Fear**

Handle the fears that can accompany new motherhood.

What scares you about motherhood? You may fear labor, delivery, an episiotomy, postpartum depression, or colic. You might be afraid that those stretch marks will never go away, that you can't handle a baby's emotions (to say nothing of your own), or that you can't figure out the logistics of a family of three. You might be afraid of your priorities changing, of going back to work, of not going back to work. You may have really big fears, like your baby won't be healthy, that you won't feel complete, or that you will mess up your child forever. Or you might be scared of the enormous responsibility.

Even if your fears are based in reality, living from fear is no life at all. Fear has the ability to hold you back. It can block your intuition and drives away faith in yourself. It can create tentative, negative, and tunnel-vision living. It can blind you from seeing possibilities for you, your baby, and your family. When you're fearful, you are hunched down with your head low, trying to stay safe. That's a very limiting place to be.

To become a mother without losing yourself, you can't allow fear to run your life. Instead, you can use fear for what it is good for—as a guide of where to put your attention and to take action. Depending on the severity of your fears and ability to overcome them, there are a variety of strategies you may want to access, from coaching to counseling to just reading a helpful book. Here are a few of our favorite fear-fighting techniques.

Shining a Light on Your Fears

To shine a light on your fear means to look at it honestly. What is this fear? What other fears are lurking nearby? Allow yourself to look inside the dark places and see what's hiding. Be painfully honest in naming your fears. Get to know them. Put them into words. You might talk them through or write them out, but become as clear and articulate about your fears as you can. Then see what happens. You may find that you feel a whole lot better.

When you shine a light on your fear, you can see it clearly. You learn to understand it. You become better informed. You see what realistically may happen and determine what's to be done. Does that mean you don't still sometimes feel afraid? No, it means that you know what to expect and have prepared yourself. Even fearful things seem less scary and more manageable in the light.

Taking Action

Taking action reduces fear and emphasizes preparation. For example, perhaps you are afraid of postpartum depression. The thought of being out of touch with yourself and your baby terrifies you, and your concerns are growing stronger every day. This is when taking action can help. You can talk to your doctor about postpartum emotions, learn the symptoms, and explore the solutions. You can also inform your husband or partner of what to look for and how to help. Just taking these few steps may allay your fears—not because postpartum depression isn't frightening, but because you've become better equipped to handle it. No matter how scary an issue seems, it almost always helps to take action. Do something about your fear and move on!

Sharing It

If there's something about motherhood that frightens you, chances are it scares everyone else. One surefire way to handle your fears is to share your fears with other expecting mothers and find out you are not alone! Talk to the women in your prenatal yoga class. Chat with a maternity ward nurse. Visit an online discussion group or talk to your mother. It can be incredibly reassuring to join a local new moms' group after the baby is born. Chances are you'll hear the same fears over and over. Just listening to other people express your fears will put them in perspective.

You may as well accept it: Being a mother can be scary. But it is also joyful beyond measure, a limitless learning experience, and tons and tons of fun! Don't let fear keep you from squeezing every ounce of juice out of your life.

CHAPTER EIGHT

Step 8
FINDING YOUR OWN SOLUTIONS

*"Find what you weren't looking for.
See what you never imagined."*
—*Kodak slogan*

Watch any new baby learn, and you'll witness a lesson in persistence. Sometimes it's difficult. Sometimes you fall down. But if you try hard enough, get creative, and ask for help when you need it, eventually you'll be able to do what you want. For your baby, that means sitting, walking, and playing. For you, it means finding solutions to life's most difficult challenges. In this chapter, you put those lessons to use to overcome your stumbling blocks.

In the last chapter you mixed reality with your ideal as you created models for your new life. You also ended up with a parking lot—a list of obstacles, questions, and things that just seem impossible. In this chapter, you get to tackle that parking lot! This is an opportunity to move past your obstacles, answer some questions, and see what is possible. It's a chance to think innovatively and experimentally—to see *how* your new life *can happen* instead of why it won't.

Whether your obstacles are small (like not knowing your company's policy on paid family leave) or more formidable (like working in a job that doesn't *have* family leave), you will learn techniques for overcoming them. So roll up your sleeves. You're about to contend with the challenges in your way.

Finding Possibilities

In this chapter you discover possible solutions for the challenges on your parking lot. Using your creativity, intuition, and resourcefulness, you move past the roadblocks between you and what you want. You experiment with a variety of problem-solving techniques like brainstorming, searching for information, and shifting your perspective. In the end, you create a possibilities chart so that you will be ready to take action in the next chapter.

Your chart may be thorough—each item from your parking lot connected to dozens of brilliant ideas for potential solutions. Or, you might include just one or two sticky obstacles with a single breakthrough idea that clears your path. You might choose to create a chart like the sample in "A Closer Look" with a box for every challenge. Some women like to use a stack of note cards with one challenge on the front and brainstormed possibilities on the back. Others choose to tack up a giant poster board with solutions scribbled and pasted all about. Feel free to take your own approach.

The possibilities on your chart are just that: possibilities. At this stage, they are not decisions or tasks to do today. Instead, your chart is a place to gather your results from using the different techniques you will learn in this chapter to see your biggest challenge in a new light. The idea is to shake up your thinking, breaking you out of feeling stuck and getting you moving again.

If your obstacle is not wanting to leave your fabulous (but tiny) downtown apartment, your possibilities might include new perspectives ("simplify!"), brainstormed ideas (get a storage unit? space-saving gadgets?), and ways to ask for what you want (like approaching building management for a larger apartment in the building). Or if your challenge is having no clue how to create a job-share situation at work, your possibilities might include contacting the human resources department or approaching a counterpart at the office to see if she might be interested in splitting a position. *You may decide not to take these routes to solutions,* but you've come up with some ideas to get you started.

The work in this chapter will help open your mind so that creative options have a chance to thrive. This ability will serve you now as you prepare for your baby and throughout your new life as a mother.

Preparing for the Obstacles Ahead

In motherhood as well as in every other area of life, challenges do indeed arise. Not only will they surface now as you're thinking about how you want your new life to be, but they are likely to keep coming through the years. When your baby is suddenly sick on the day you have a big presentation at work, has hit a new developmental milestone and is no longer satisfied with any of the toys or activities you offer, or in any number of other tests on your patience, the ability to see possibilities and search for creative solutions will serve you well. Obstacles will still arise, but you can learn how to prevent them from stopping you. Instead of feeling stuck or limited, you can learn to feel optimistic and courageous. Perhaps there are ways around, through, or over your obstacles that will keep you moving in the direction of your dreams. All it takes is learning how to find new perspectives, becoming more open to the possibilities, and finding the willingness to ask for what you need.

In some cases, challenges may not change, but your thinking can. You can use the skill of changing your viewpoint to see the solution differently—to learn to accept the way things are and work *with* them instead of *against* them. This is especially helpful when challenges really are immovable. Here are some examples.

- Amanda's husband lost his job in her fourth month of pregnancy.
- JoAnn found out she was having twins.
- BJ's adoption agency called with a baby for them to bring home *that very day*.

The challenges for these women took on a new urgency. In these cases, the mothers learned to change their perspective instead of the circumstances. Their questions shifted from "How can I make this situation *change"* to "How can I make this situation *work?* What will it take for me to rise to this occasion?" Use the strategies in this chapter to not only deal with your obstacles, but also your own perceptions so you can make almost any situation a success.

So get ready to charge, jump, and soar past what's between you and your ideal life as a mother.

"Changing my perspective was fundamental for me to become pregnant in the first place. I'm 40 and was convinced that it was going to be terribly difficult to conceive. I had heard so many sad stories of endless fertility treatments and failed pregnancies that I was stressed before we even started trying. The shift came when I started thinking the opposite, that it's easy to get pregnant, because for some people that is true. I know my thinking might have had nothing to do with it, but I like to believe that is when I actually conceived!"   —ELISE, 5 MONTHS PREGNANT

FINDING YOUR OWN WAY
Generating Possibilities

There are a host of techniques you can use to find possible solutions for your challenges. The exercises in the next two sections are tools that you can use now and throughout your new life.

To begin, take out your parking lot. Review your obstacles. Revisit your questions. Remind yourself of what feels impossible. Choose one to focus on now. You will try different techniques to address this issue as thoroughly as possible, in hopes that you resolve it. Even if you don't, you will become open to a solution revealing itself in the future. Commit to this one challenge for now. You don't have to solve all of your problems today. Write down your choice on a piece of paper.

Read through the different exercises below and try one or more. Feel free to use the worksheets in "A Closer Look" to organize your efforts or just some blank sheets of paper; be sure to keep track of your ideas in the "My Possibility Chart" in the "Keepsakes" section at the back of the book. These techniques aren't new or complicated. What's new is that you're applying them *now,* in service of your approaching motherhood and creating your ideal life. You will be accessing your own creativity and resources, bringing them to bear on your challenge to see if any new ideas become available.

Brainstorming. In some cases, you are your own best resource. You have been solving problems your whole life; this challenge does not need to be different. Think about how you usually brainstorm ideas. Perhaps you like to scribble down a bunch of ideas on a piece of paper. Some women like to think in the shower or mull things over with their partner or a good friend. The key is to create an environment conducive to free thinking, taking care to leave fear and doubt behind.

Rachel described her obstacle this way: "We still have huge student loans from graduate school, along with everything else. So now we're highly, highly overextended financially. It would be impossible to have the opportunity to take a year off with the baby." Rachel wanted to brainstorm ideas with her husband, George. They decided to talk about ideas while walking their favorite hiking trail. The change of pace and spring sunshine as well as a more relaxed mood facilitated the conversation. Rachel and George came up with several potential solutions.

- Refinance the house for lower payments.
- Keep the house but trade in the cars for used, economical ones.

- Make some sacrifices to take a good maternity leave then continue working full-time to afford everything we've got; it's worth it.

- Ask George's boss for a raise (the worst he can say is no!).

- Sell some of our investments to cover costs the first year so I can cut back on work; we'll be investing in our lives instead of in the stock market!

Do your own brainstorming now or commit to a time, day, and great location for finding new possibilities. Keep track of any ideas you come up with for resolving the challenges you face.

Brainstorming is all about generating as many ideas as possible—let them flow.

Searching for Information. Don't hesitate to do your research. Maybe no one has been in your shoes, but millions of women have been in their *own* shoes with similar challenges. You can ask a friend if he or she has any ideas, or ask an expert like a lactation consultant, an experienced mother, or a human resources representative at work. You can browse the bookshelves at the nearest bookstore or library or simply hop on the Internet. Know that something has been written about almost every single issue known to womankind.

Jen picked some questions for her challenge. "What if I am back at work and realize my childcare options aren't working? Will I have to go to half-time? And does that financially work out right? Will my salary be eaten up by the amount of money we put into childcare?" Using the worksheet in "A Closer Look" as a guide, Jen listed research strategies that would help in her search for answers. Jen settled on the following ideas as next steps to resolve her challenge:

- Get three to five childcare plans that actually work from my friends with kids.

- Go back to budget modeling and run the numbers. Get the facts about how much money I would have to make to cover the costs of childcare with enough money left over to make it "worth it."

- Check out five different childcare options (home care, small private daycare, large school-like setting, babysitter, nanny) to compare costs.

The act of calmly making a list of research tasks can take the drama out of seemingly difficult obstacles. List your ideas for inquiring into your challenges. See how your thinking opens up.

Making Requests. If you know what you want but doubt you can have it, think of asking directly for what you need. Make a list of requests—whether it's asking your husband or partner to cut back on business travel, asking your friends to make meals for the first few weeks, or asking your boss for a laptop to use at home. Stop assuming the answer is no and see if you might find a yes, a maybe, or even a no-but-here's-what-I-can-do.

Connie described a difficult challenge, "My husband has health issues that make it hard for me to be able to count on his help." Taking a fresh approach, she contemplated what she could ask for to better deal with this formidable obstacle. Connie was pleased to find several requests she could try.

- To her husband: "Will you help out more with the baby when you're feeling strong so that I can take over when you're not?"

- To her boss: "Can we discuss contingency plans for the days my husband has to go back to the hospital?"

- To her husband's doctor: "Will you refer us to a counseling group that can help us get support during this difficult time?"

- To the baby: "Will you love us even though we can't always be there for you when we want to? (I know the baby can't answer, but just asking this question helps me imagine its answer will be, 'of course!')"

Now take one of your obstacles and consider who can really help you. Make a list of exactly what you would ask for and imagine making all those requests. Notice how your obstacle feels now.

Each technique brings you another step closer to what you desire. As you work, note each possible solution or idea that you find for successfully resolving a challenge or answering a question. In the next chapter you will use some or all of these ideas as part of your plan to take action.

KEEPSAKE

Copy each challenge and new idea for moving forward under "My Possibilities Chart" in the "Keepsakes" section in Appendix A or in your own journal or notebook.

FINDING YOUR OWN WAY
Opening Your Mind

The quest for possibilities also includes opening your mind and shifting your perspective so your challenges don't seem as daunting. This is an invaluable technique that can work wonders. Pick another item from your parking lot or use the same challenge from before to play with the suggestions below. Remember that you can use the worksheets and extra help in "A Closer Look" at the end of the chapter and keep track of your ideas in the "My Possibility Chart" in the "Keepsakes" section at the back of the book.

Reframing Your Challenge as a Question. Even if your parking lot item is an obstacle or impossibility, state it now as a question. This alone may move you a step closer to seeing possibilities, since questions can be answered, whereas statements seem so final.

Go ahead. Try rewording your choice as a question. Write it down.

For example, Tammy chose this obstacle from her parking lot: "I can't keep doing everything I've been doing." She knew she needed to dig her way out of her deep involvement at work, with her friends, and her community obligations. She restated her challenge as the question: "How do I stop myself from being all things to all people?"

Randi had questions around the logistics of feeding her baby. She planned to breastfeed, but also badly wanted to pursue a once-in-a-lifetime opportunity to take an overseas account. She knew she could pump her milk so others could feed her son while she traveled on business but didn't know logistically how that would really work. Her questions included "How can I pump enough?" "When do I pump?" "How does pumping fit with this kind of travel?" Randi recast these as a single question: "How can I successfully breastfeed my son, even if I'm traveling overseas once a month?"

Kanna wanted her first weeks after delivery to be just her, her husband, and their baby. Her obstacle was the fact her due date was December 12 and all the relatives wanted to come for the holidays to see the baby. Kanna's question was "How do I get my relatives to stay away without alienating them?"

Look at the question you wrote for your challenge. Read it out loud. Forming your challenge in the shape of a question may not bring you the answers you want right away, but it can make you more open to finding them.

Shifting from Closed and Blocked to Receptive and Open. The next step is to move from any feelings of being stuck ("I have no options") to a mindset that moves you forward ("I know there are a limitless variety of options"). To do this, check out how you are feeling. Ask yourself:

❓ How am I currently thinking about this challenge?

❓ What's the little voice in my head saying?

❓ How does it make me feel to think this way?

Write down any thoughts and emotions. This is your current perspective on the issue. Notice how your body reacts to this perspective. Are you standing up straight, lounging, hunched over, tense, or relaxed? Your perspective can affect everything about you.

Now even if it is difficult, imagine that there's a different way of thinking about this challenge. You don't have to actually change your mind, but just experiment to see what other viewpoints are available. One easy way to do this is to look for the polar opposite of your current mindset. If your thinking is, "This is too hard for me to figure out," the opposite would be, "This is easy for me to figure out." If your thinking is, "There's no way for me to have what I want," try thinking, "There are several ways for me to have what I want." This can feel awkward at first if you are accustomed to accepting the negative perspective as truth.

On your sheet of paper, write down the opposite perspective. What does it feel like to think from this vantage point? What's different?

Expanding Your Perspective. Continue looking for additional perspectives. Consider what someone else would think about your challenge. This helps you see that somewhere out there in the universe there must be another way, even if it's not for you. Imagine how a friend, colleague, your husband or partner, or even a character on your favorite television show would view your challenge. You can try using a metaphor to twist your thinking—if you're feeling like a lump of mud in your current perspective, try imagining the perspective of a crashing wave or a leaf in the wind.

Look at Tammy's challenge again: "How do I stop myself from being all things to all people?" Even after rewording her challenge as a question, Tammy felt it was impossible to extract herself from the important roles she fulfilled in her own life and the lives of others. She tried to imagine how other people would answer the question like her easy-going best friend, then her calm and collected mother, and finally her very balanced boss. It suddenly dawned on Tammy that none of these people were trying to juggle everything she was. Maybe doing less was actually possible. With this shift of perspective, Tammy felt for the first time that maybe she could let go of some responsibilities.

Now you try. Choose a few people and think of how they might view your challenge. Write down at least two new perspectives on your sheet of paper.

Finding New Possibilities. The point of this exercise is to open your eyes to the possibilities around you. If you stay attached to your original point of view, you virtually guarantee you'll stay stuck. However, if you realize there are different ways of looking at your situation, you are already advancing toward the life you want.

Review the perspectives that you wrote down on your sheet of paper. Which one appeals to you? What possibilities do you see if you take that perspective? Pick a new way of looking at your obstacle and write down any ideas that emerge about resolving your challenge.

If you want more practice in shifting your perspective, there is a step-by-step exercise in "A Closer Look" to guide you to new ways of thinking.

KEEPSAKE

Copy your challenge and any ideas for solutions under "My Possibilities Chart" in the "Keepsakes" section in Appendix A or in your own journal or notebook.

TIPS FOR OPENING YOUR MIND

- Physically shift your perspective—lie down, walk outside, go for a drive!
- Nothing is too wild—try thinking from your pet's perspective or yourself twenty years from now.
- Have fun! Lighten up!

Common Experiences

Putting effort into overcoming your obstacles can be positive, productive work. Not only does it help you break through to what you really want, it can also bring you new tools, abilities, and confidence in leading an empowered life. Here are some other women's experiences as they worked on their challenges.

Breaking Through. The best-case scenario in finding possible solutions occurs when it leads to a breakthrough! One of the most striking examples of this happened to Melinda, a marketing consultant who shifted her perspective in a significant way. Melinda's biggest obstacle was her work. She had an extremely full calendar when she learned she was pregnant; she had booked clients through the end of the year, and then found out she would be giving birth in the fall! Panicked, she could not see a way out of her scheduling issue short of quitting her business entirely. She was sure her clients would all leave if she told them she would need time off for maternity leave. Deep down, she thought, "I'm only valuable when I'm working."

Forced to rethink this perspective, she slowly formed the words that would represent an opposite viewpoint: "I am even more valuable when I'm not working."

Melinda paused. Simply saying the words got her started; it took her brain a few moments to catch up. Then she realized that she would be more valuable to the baby when she wasn't working . . . and she would be more valuable to her clients when she returned to work if she was truly rested and adjusted to her new life.

In her next steps, Melinda was able to move from closed ("There's no way I can take a maternity leave") to open ("How can I take a maternity leave?") to strategic ("What have other consultants done when they've had babies? How did they negotiate their maternity leaves with their clients?"). Melinda's ability to shift her perspective with an open mind allowed her to put together a plan that was right for her, her baby, and her business.

Getting Great Ideas. No matter what obstacle you might be working on, the process of working through it can bring you great ideas in a number of areas. One of Hope's obstacles was her lack of knowledge about childcare. She had reframed the obstacle into a question: "What do you think is the best way to care for a baby?" She then committed to asking six people:

- Her best friend

- A woman she knew who adopted three kids

- A mom who started her baby in daycare but switched to being a stay-at-home mother

- Her 83-year-old aunt who had raised eight children

- Another relative who was a nanny

- A friend who had a miscarriage and then adopted a baby

Hope found what she expected, a lot of heart-warming advice as well as conflicting opinions. What she didn't expect was how wonderful it felt to have an excuse to connect with these women and how pleased they were to be asked their opinion and to be admired as mothers. In the end, Hope did take one piece of advice from the adoptive mother who told her to stop asking for advice and to follow her heart! "This gave me the permission and validation for me to trust my own instincts." The process of asking for help with her obstacles yielded a whole lot of added advantages.

Welcoming Openness and Possibility. Freedom. Relief. Delight. These are just some of the reactions that women experience by shifting their perspective. Lauren found a release of anxiety in making the shift from "I need to work hard at my job" to "I need to work hard at getting ready for the baby." Sylvia experienced a new sense of playfulness when she used metaphors to rethink her obstacle of decreased energy in her last trimester. She considered her lethargy from the perspective of a floating balloon and then a butterfly. She moved from feeling pressured and inadequate to feeling "relaxed, as if I can just go with the flow of the air currents, unhurried, natural, and easy-going." A sense of openness and possibility is one of the hallmarks of the perspective shift.

Finding the Beauty in the Barriers. In the case of really stubborn obstacles, you may need persistence, supported by a positive mindset, to see how you can eliminate what stands in your way. For instance, when Katherine finally found the perfect home daycare, she faced an extremely stubborn obstacle: The babysitter only worked four days a week. Nothing about this situation would change; either Katherine had to find a way to work with it or keep looking for another daycare. She brainstormed every option she could think of, including hiring a separate babysitter for Fridays, using her parents once a week, using her church's preschool, and she and her partner's taking every other Friday off. She even asked the other moms at the daycare if they could take her son on Fridays. In the end, all of Katherine's exploration seemed to be pointing to one reality: She was going to have to take Fridays off.

Katherine agreed to try looking at this situation from a more positive perspective. For a week, she tried believing, "I *get* to take Fridays off." Then a funny thing happened—the idea started to grow on her. She felt a little tickled, like she was skipping school. For the first time in her working life she had an excuse for taking a break! Three years later as her son went off to preschool, Katherine laughed as she recalled the difficulty she had making the decision to work only four days a week. "It really never affected my work and it was a marvelous time with my son. My whole life I will remember the good times we had on Fridays in my son's first three years of life." Sometimes what at first appears to be an obstacle turns out to be a blessing.

Finding an Opportunity for Partnership. Many women experience a breakthrough when they remember they're not alone. Kay had trouble overcoming the feeling that she wouldn't be contributing equally with her husband once she went on maternity leave. She saw this as an opportunity to team up with her husband so they could work together to shift her perspective. "I had a good talk with Jason about this. One perspective we came to was this. *We both will still be working*—in different locations like we do now—each day. He will be at the office, and I will be working at home taking care of the baby. In the evening, taking care of our home will be *both* our responsibilities as it has always been. The only difference is our responsibilities will now include our daughter." Bringing in a partner to help find potential solutions can be a fruitful way to create the life you want.

From Stumbling Blocks to Stepping Stones

By this point in the process of *Becoming a Mother,* you have achieved a remarkable feat! You have boldly faced some of your most difficult challenges. Our hope is that you are seeing possibilities where once you saw only barriers and that now you know the life of your dreams is a life you can create.

In this chapter, you have tackled some of the stumbling blocks in your way. You have broken out of closed ways of thinking. You have practiced creative methods of problem solving that you can use to overcome the hardest parts of changing your life.

We acknowledge that this is a process—one that takes time, effort, and persistence. It's not always easy to work on obstacles. At times it can be easier to just stay stuck. You may have to keep playing with your stumbling blocks to get the results you want. But you will see the results if you stay committed and true to yourself. Don't be surprised if those stumbling blocks eventually become stepping stones on your road to becoming the kind of mother you want to be.

An Inquiry for You	What am I stepping into?

C O N G R A T U L A T I O N S !

You have just completed one of the most difficult and powerful steps toward creating your new life—learning to overcome your challenges. We want to acknowledge you for

- Bravely facing your questions, obstacles, and seeming impossibilities.
- Considering different perspectives.
- Finding new ways to problem solve.
- Creating possibilities.

A Closer Look

To help you deal with your parking lot, we have included many resources. First, you will find a more detailed exercise to help you shift your perspective, followed by a set of worksheets you can use for each problem-solving technique and finally, a sample of one mom-to-be's chart of possibilities. We suggest reviewing all of these now, as they may help you create your own possibilities.

Exercise: Shifting Your Perspective

In *Becoming a Mother,* we have great faith in the ability of a perspective shift to generate ideas for solutions. In this exercise we walk you through the process step by step so you will have this tool to help you throughout your new life.

• **Identifying your current perspective.** Write down the challenge you are working with at the top of a piece of paper. You also can use the "Perpective Shift" worksheet following this exercise as a guide. (It may be helpful to look at it now to get a sense of how this exercise works.)

Feel and think about how you currently look at this obstacle or issue. This is Perspective 1. What's going through your head about this challenge? What's your inner dialogue like? How does it make you feel to think this way? Notice your body language when you think from this perspective. Usually, this first perspective is a pretty negative one. Don't try to shift into another perspective too quickly. Just wallow around in this one until you really *feel* this viewpoint.

Once you have the feeling, write down a name for this perspective on your worksheet or paper. Write a description in some detail, explaining what this perspective is like for you. Fill in the sentence, "I feel _____ in this perspective." Identify a few key words for the emotions that this viewpoint makes you feel.

Example: Georgia picked "being at home alone with the baby" as her obstacle. Although she was thrilled about the baby coming, Georgia was afraid she would feel isolated and

EXTRA RESOURCES

Electronic versions of all the worksheets in this chapter are available at **www.empoweredmotherhood.com,** plus a special digital recording of us coaching you through the perspective exercise.

lonely taking care of the baby, and this worried her. She started by writing down "I will be isolated" as Perspective 1. When she really thought about it honestly, Georgia acknowledged she was feeling a lot of negative emotions at the moment—she wrote down anger, fear, panic, frustration, and resentment. Her description of the perspective also included "there will only be me at home every day to figure it out." Her stomach hurt just thinking about it, and she felt like lashing out at someone. If she closed her eyes, she imagined it all looked like red heat sparks coming off her body. Georgia summed it up with "I feel scared and resentful."

- **Seeing what's possible from your current perspective.** What's possible from this first perspective? If it is a negative or hopeless perspective, your answer might be that "nothing," "paralysis," or "inaction" is possible! If it's a positive perspective, you might feel that "movement" or even "breakthrough" is possible. The idea is to see how this particular perspective affects what you think is possible.

Georgia thought about what was possible from her perspective of "I will be isolated." She thought about the worst case. If she continued to have a perspective of fear about staying at home with the baby, her maternity leave started to look desolate. What seemed possible was that she could see herself trapped in a cycle of worry.

- **Inventing another perspective.** Look for another perspective. Start by physically moving from wherever you are; get up and literally find another viewpoint. Walk into another room or step outside. Change your position—stretch out, curl up, look out the window, or turn around. Change *something* to help change your point of view, to see the world from a different angle—a move that may free up new ways of seeing your obstacle.

This physical change might be enough to trigger another perspective on your challenge. If not, look around and see if anything nearby gives you an idea. If nothing comes, try these questions. What is the opposite viewpoint from Perspective 1? What would the baby's perspective on the obstacle be? How about other people you know or know of, maybe someone famous or that you admire? What about the perspective from a different place—your viewpoint if you were on top of a mountain, in the ocean, on the edge of a volcano, or lying in a flower-filled garden? The places to look are endless—grab anything as long as it differs than your first perspective.

Remember, you do not have to change your mind about how you look at your obstacle. You are welcome to return your original perspective if you like. All you are doing now is stretching your mind.

Take your new perspective and go through the same reflection as you did with your first. How do you see your obstacle now? What do you feel like physically and emotionally in this perspective? What name would you give this viewpoint? Write it all down under Perspective 2 on your worksheet or paper.

As you did before, ask yourself what's possible from this perspective. It may be something different than last time!

Georgia got up and left the kitchen. She ambled into the baby's room and sat in the rocker. She thought about "being alone at home with the baby" again. The perspective she wrote down was "it will be cozy and comfortable, a nice little nest." Georgia described the feeling, "This is my safe place, it has everything I need." She felt physically calmer with this viewpoint, more objective, less dramatic. When she closed her eyes, she imagined yellow sunshine—nurturing and energizing. She sat up and wrote, "I feel relaxed and confident in this perspective." Then she thought about what was possible from this new perspective. Her reaction was very different from before. "I can experience taking care of my baby, focus on what's going on with her, and be curious."

- **Find more perspectives.** Do it again! This is the important step. Even if you are excited and already feeling a shift in your thinking, keep going! Magic happens when you move past two perspectives. It's as if your brain suddenly gets the hang of it and realizes you are seriously willing to open and shift. So get up and move again. Be as free in your thinking as possible. Gather as many different perspectives as you can. Write down all the information for each new perspective you find. Don't forget to consider what's possible from each perspective.

This time Georgia walked outside onto her deck. The sun was going down and the neighborhood was quiet. As she breathed deep a few times, the perspective that came to her was, "Alone time is powerful." She saw it as positive energy filling up a balloon. This perspective felt strong and she described it as "I can conquer anything I want to. I can do it." Georgia wrote, "I feel empowered." She realized that a lot was possible from this perspective, "I can take on things I've been afraid of, not just about the baby."

- **Choosing a perspective.** We want you to feel the power of choice. Decide how you're going to think about your obstacle. You have several perspectives to choose from. You can keep your original viewpoint or choose something else. For each perspective you're considering, remember to ask yourself, *will this help me create the life I want?*

Take a moment to walk through and review each of the perspectives. Read each one and remember what it felt like. Then choose one, even if it is just to try on for a while. Choose a perspective to hold for the rest of the day or the next week. Choose the one that feels most right to you—the one that is closely aligned with your values, beliefs, and intention for your new life as a mother. You might end up combining some elements of a few of your perspectives. Whatever you choose, consciously take on that new point of view.

Thinking from your chosen viewpoint, see what possible solutions are available to you. How could your perceived obstacle be overcome by thinking from this new vantage point? Write your ideas down at the bottom of your worksheet. Remember that no matter what, you always have the power to choose your perspective.

Georgia laughed when she looked back at her original perspective. Even though Georgia could see that she had been pessimistic, it had felt so real at the time. She chose Perspective 3, "Alone time is powerful." Georgia felt excited and thought about the possibilities for her new life with a baby. The obstacle was no longer there; being alone with the baby just didn't seem so scary any more.

Be sure to add your ideas to "My Possibilities Chart" in the "Keepsakes" section in Appendix A.

<u>*Worksheet*</u>
My Brainstorm

My Challenge: _____

The possibilities this opens up for me are:

Be sure to add your ideas to "My Possibilities Chart" in the "Keepsakes" section in Appendix A.

Worksheet
My Search for Information

My Challenge:

Questions:

1.

2.

3.

4.

5.

6.

7.

People to Talk To	**Websites**	**Other Resources**
_____	_____	_____
_____	_____	_____
_____	_____	_____
_____	_____	_____
_____	_____	_____

The possibilities this opens up for me are:

Be sure to add your ideas to "My Possibilities Chart" in the "Keepsakes" section in Appendix A.

<u>*Worksheet*</u>
Making Requests

My Challenge:

Request 1:

Request 2:

Request 3:

Request 4:

Request 5:

The possibilities now are:

Be sure to add your ideas to "My Possibilities Chart" in the "Keepsakes" section in Appendix A.

Worksheet
Perspective Shift

My Challenge:

Perspective 1: _____

Description _____

_____

I feel _____ in this perspective.

What's possible from this perspective? _____

Perspective 2: _____

Description _____

_____

I feel _____ in this perspective.

What's possible from this perspective? _____

Perspective 3: _____

Description _____

_____

I feel _____ in this perspective.

What's possible from this perspective? _____

Perspective 4: _____

Description _____

_____

I feel _____ in this perspective.

What's possible from this perspective? _____

Perspective 5: _____

Description _____

_____

I feel _____ in this perspective.

What's possible from this perspective? _____

My Choice:

The perspective I choose to hold on the subject of _____ is:

The possibilities this opens up for me are:

Be sure to add your ideas to "My Possibilities Chart" in the "Keepsakes" section in Appendix A.

Sample "My Possibilities Chart"

Challenge: *Money (How can we afford this lifestyle with a new baby?)*

Possibilities:

- *Ask for a raise (me, Andy)*
- *Research fun "side jobs"*
- *Track budget; see where we can rearrange expenses*

Challenge: *Getting Enough Help (What can Andy reasonably do?)*

Possibilities:

- *Assume he wants to help!!*
- *Most important: evening dinner/dishes*
- *Neighbor's son (Nick?) to walk Bruno*
- *Brainstorm with Andy on who else can help (cleaning service? Lisa?)*

Challenge: *ROOM!!! (How can we all fit in this apartment?)*

Possibilities:

- *At least explore the idea of a bigger apartment*
- *Storage unit?*
- *Keep it simple with baby "stuff"; start small*

Lessons in BECOMING A MOTHER

Lesson 8 **The Gift of Gratitude**

Find joy in any circumstance.

So much is extraordinary about having a baby. The mysterious wisdom of your pregnant body. Your baby's rapid growth from a microscopic dot on the screen to a fully formed little person. The miracle of birth. When you feel your baby move, you may be overcome with wonder of this tiny being within and filled with gratitude for the experience. At times like this, you feel blessed indeed.

Feeling grateful is easy when you're overcome with joy. It's a skill to feel grateful when you're *not*. Whether you're battling first-trimester exhaustion, third-trimester insomnia, or the stress of an upcoming life change, you might find yourself grumpy and irritable. That feeling may carry into the early weeks of having a baby as you adjust to your new life.

As you shift from expecting mama to hands-on mama, the gift of gratitude can turn any not-so-perfect scenario into practically paradise. If you can be grateful in the moment, suddenly incessant crying becomes a sign of vitality. Those endless dirty diapers represent the miracle of a brand-new, fully functioning human body. Even arguments with your loved ones when your nerves are shot can become a reminder that you're not alone. It's not living in a fantasy to appreciate the glory of your life. It's not pretending. It's choosing to be content, even in an imperfect world.

Gratitude cultivates happiness. No matter what circumstances you're in, no matter how close or far you feel to the ideal life you want to create, being grateful for what you do have can make you feel that your life is very near perfect.

The shift from grumpiness to gratitude is a conscious skill and one worth having. Start practicing gratitude now! Here are a few suggestions to help.

Comparing Down and Back, Not Up and Out

No matter how abundant your life is, it can seem paltry compared to someone else's if that someone else appears to have more than you. Comparing your life now to the life you really want can also cause dissatisfaction. The best path to gratitude is to drop comparisons altogether. However, if you must compare, try comparing your life to where you've been and to where you've thankfully never had to be. Remember a time when you were really struggling and think of how much you have grown since then. Consider what your life would be like if you lived in true poverty or oppression. Suddenly you have plenty to be grateful for. Your baby will be coming into life with incredible blessings. Recognize it.

Focusing on the Details

Noticing the details of life is a little game that can help you experience gratitude. It shows you the delightful and staggering abundance of goodness in life. Sara practiced gratitude this way one night while she soothed her son for the umpteenth time. She decided to be grateful for everything she could see from her rocking chair. She spotted the photo of her son's precious face on the day of his baptism, a memory that would be with her forever. The music playing that comforted both her and her baby. The soft color of yellow light glowing gently in the dark. The socks in her son's drawer to keep him warm, the wipes on the shelf to keep him clean, the water in her glass that was safe to drink. Twenty minutes later, she was still finding things to treasure. Every moment is overflowing with the details that make up life. Notice them, and you'll experience gratitude.

Finding Value in Discontent

This skill is an escape route out of self-pity. It means noticing when you're dwelling on the negative and choosing to be grateful for it instead. For instance, let's say you're struggling with the financial pressures of having a baby. Gratitude is to be thankful for those financial pressures, for they're helping you rethink your life and forcing you to rearrange your priorities. Or maybe your doctor put you on bed rest. In the midst of the boredom and discomfort, gratitude means being thankful for the opportunity to protect and save the life of your baby. Not every mother has that chance. Plus, you get to do it with books to read (be thankful for your literacy), the company of others (be thankful for their support), and the care of a doctor (be thankful for quality healthcare). The difficulties in life can connect you to gratitude in a deep and meaningful way, helping you to get through them, and yes, even be thankful.

The gift of gratitude, sincerely felt, can transform your world before your eyes. Even the darkest hour becomes a marvel. We're not saying you will always feel like being grateful. Sometimes what you need is a good cry or the chance to whine. Go for it. Sometimes that helps, too. But when you're searching for a life that brings you happiness, contentment, and peace, gratitude can show that you're already there.

CHAPTER NINE

Step 9
MAKING COMMITMENTS
AND TAKING ACTION

*"Vision without action is merely dreaming. Action with no vision
is just passing time.
But with vision and action you can change the world."*
—*Nelson Mandela*

Imagine actually living the ideal life you've envisioned, *today*—the one that brings out your best as a woman and as a mother. You have chosen what you want. You have identified your catalysts—those few key changes that will have lasting impact. You have mapped out what your new life might look like and worked to move past obstacles and questions. Now it's time to live it.

In this chapter, you take action. It's time to start making the changes you've identified. *Now* is the time to live your ideal life. You know what you want; why wait? You have the chance to make your new life real—not when your baby arrives, but right now—by taking the steps that will bring your vision to life.

New motherhood is all about new life—not just your baby's life, but your own.

Taking Action

Until now, you have been focusing on life after the baby is born, because that is when your life will *really* change. But you can start living your new life now. That way, when your baby arrives, you will be more at ease and better able to deal with any emotions, events, or energy that pulls or pushes you away from the life you want to live.

In this chapter, you jump-start your new life by choosing items from your prioritized list and putting them into place. In other words, you create an action plan and get to work! Your action plan contains specific, realistic actions that you are willing to commit to and make your top priority. By doing so, you will be announcing that you are indeed changing your life for the sake of yourself as a woman and mother, as well as for your baby and husband or partner.

Choosing an item from your prioritized list sets the tone. Some women choose a catalyst that is very concrete. For example, Jenna selected her "help at home" catalyst and Margaret picked "a shorter commute." Other women choose something more abstract like Kyla's taking "positive home environment"—a commitment to be more cheerful and optimistic at home. We encourage you to start with your biggest catalysts, because those are the ones that will create the greatest impact in your life!

Moving into action doesn't have to be complicated. Ideas for next steps can be straightforward and simple. The point is to discover those steps that are doable *now*. For example, Vanessa's catalyst was "sleep support." Vanessa felt that if she could find a way to get a little extra snooze time, as a new mom she would be more able to cope, love, and be thoughtful in her new life. Her ideas for actions to guarantee sleep included:

1. Create a list of people who can come over while I nap.
2. Talk to Jack about sharing nighttime feedings.
3. Ask my sister to be on the lookout for me after the baby is born and raise a red flag if it looks like I'm losing my mind.
4. Sign people up now to help me with the baby in those first couple of weeks so I don't lose too much sleep in the first place.

These were all actions that Vanessa felt she could easily and happily do right away.

The most important part of taking action is making the commitment. You don't have to overhaul your entire life all at once. Just get started by taking one or two steps today. You are making a huge difference in yourself psychologically and energetically just by claiming what you want through taking action now. You are communicating your intent to make a change and moving in the right direction.

"I need to get real about how imminent this change in my life is. The stakes have been raised! If I want more balance in my life because I want to be a more relaxed, go-with-the-flow, roll-with-the-punches kind of new mother, then I need to make some decisions now to get that balance! If I don't, I need to see what I am really sacrificing—not just my peace of mind, but the whole way I want my life to be."
—OLIVIA, 6 MONTHS PREGNANT

The Wow of Now

The advantage of taking action now is that when the baby does come, you can focus all of your attention on him or her. You probably won't be too keen on rethinking your entire life when you have a brand new baby at home. You can become the woman and mother you want to be *now*, so that this will be the mother and life waiting for your baby. Each step you take makes your new life real, whether it is booking a massage appointment for two months after your due date, dropping out of that committee, or lining up your babysitters. Taking action builds your confidence, energizes, and empowers you. You will create the momentum that has life already flowing the way you want, even before your baby is born.

Here's an example. Michele's catalyst was to "take a *real* maternity leave." As the owner of a home business, it seemed almost impossible for her to step away for six months. She took a small step two months before the baby was due: cutting back on the hours spent dealing with email. Michele started by unsubscribing to her electronic newsletters. Then she nicely asked friends to take her off their email distribution lists. It was hard at first to just do it, and she worried that she might miss something critical. But after a week or two, the emails stopped coming and her inbox was cut in half. This simple step freed up extra time for Michele to enjoy her last few months of pregnancy. It also boosted her confidence to eliminate her work-related emails altogether, helping her take those six months off from work.

Taking action now also helps ensure success in putting your new life into place. Jackie started doling out her work projects three months before her maternity leave was to start, telling people that she wanted to give them the chance to take over while she was still available to help. When Jackie's doctor unexpectedly prescribed her bed rest, she was truly able to leave work behind and focus on staying healthy and relaxed. If she hadn't started taking action early, she would have been torn between putting her colleagues in a bind or having to field work calls when she was supposed to be resting.

> *"So many people have been telling me what motherhood will be or mean to me, what I will experience, what I will feel, do, and even think. Now, I get to decide who I will be as a mother, what I want to do. I get to actively choose and plan rather than sit back and accept what others tell me to do or be. This process has given me more control and permission to do what's right for me. It's made everything less scary."*
> —KAREN, 8 MONTHS PREGNANT

Change takes time. You are forming new habits, rearranging your time, making new kinds of decisions and doing things in new ways. The sooner you start, the more comfortable and consistent you will be in creating the kind of life that honors you and your family—not once, but every day.

FINDING YOUR OWN WAY
Taking Action

Step up! Commit to your new life for you and your family by taking action *today*. Now is your opportunity to bring everything together. You will create your action plan to propel you forward and determine how to keep yourself on track. Remember, your action plan doesn't have to be a list, especially if you hate that approach. There are dozens of other formats for action plans, some of which are very creative. In "A Closer Look" at the end of this chapter, we offer you some ideas for coming up with an action plan that will inspire and motivate you along with a sample of a traditional plan. If you have been working with your husband or partner, this is a great step to take together.

Finding Your Focus. Choose where to focus your energy by picking a single item from your prioritized list. Any item will do, but consider your catalysts. We want you to see powerful results and feel the exhilaration of creating change that is aligned with your values, beliefs, and intention.

If you are feeling tentative, try viewing this exercise as a dry run, an experiment, just practice. Shrug off any pressure you may be feeling. Let go of any fear or insecurity. Don't be overwhelmed by everything you need to do—that's why you focus on only one thing for now.

Be bold! Don't hold back! Get out your list and pick the item that will make the most significant impact in your life. Write it down on a piece of paper.

Generating Potential Actions. Brainstorm potential actions to bring your item into reality. Let the ideas flow for realistic, doable first steps. Look at the chart of possibilities you created when working on your obstacles, see what actions you already identified. Then ask yourself these questions:

> ❷ What actions can I take *this* week?

> ❷ If this was my ONLY priority today, what would I do first?

> ❷ If I believed with all my heart that this item was the key to my new life, how would I get started?

Write down your ideas. Don't just think of the actions that *could* be done, but the kinds of actions you *will* do. Small steps are fine. However, if you come up with a spine-tingling leap to take, that's brilliant, too! Make sure it is something that you can actually do.

If you are stuck, use any of the techniques from the previous chapter—brainstorming, researching information, and making requests—to produce more ideas for action. Another approach is to think about the resources available to you such as time, money, friends, colleagues, skills, and special talents. You probably have more at your disposal than you realize. Add any actions that take advantage of your resources to your list.

Committing. Identify the actions *you will actually commit to today*. By today, we mean that you…

- Can START each action in the next seven days (today if you wish).
- Have the ability to take these actions.
- Have the time and opportunity to take these actions.

Don't take on too much. At this point, you do not need actions for everything on your prioritized list. You may choose to commit to a single action; that's fine. The important thing is that you can *do* it. For example, Pam brainstormed a few actions for her catalyst—making sure her husband Danny would still feel special after the baby arrived. Her light bulb idea was to buy tickets for Danny and his father to go to a Dodger's baseball game—three months from now for Father's Day. Danny hadn't gone to a game with his father for ten years and Pam knew the gift would thrill both of them. This was an action she could easily take today—Pam was elated by finding an action she could move on before the baby arrived.

Go ahead and circle the actions you commit to.

Holding Yourself Accountable. Finally, before you take action, set up some accountability to strengthen your commitment to action. Be even more specific about your commitment, identifying not just what you will do but *when* you are going to do it and *how* you will prove it. Sometimes putting your commitment in writing is enough. However, consider setting external accountability for your actions—asking your husband or partner, a friend, or a personal coach to follow up with you to see how you are doing on your commitment. If nothing else, take the time to communicate what you're up to with someone you trust.

Melissa held herself accountable by ensuring she couldn't back out of her commitment to the catalyst of "a real maternity leave." She changed her voice mail message three weeks before the baby was due. Instead of inviting everyone who called to "leave your name and number so I can call you back," she created a message that said, "Thank you for calling. I am currently on maternity leave and will be unavailable for phone calls until I return." The people she loved knew how to get in touch with her, and everyone else got the hint. Melissa told her husband to not let her change the message back until after her maternity leave was over!

Strengthen your commitment. Ask yourself:

❷ When will I do these actions?

❷ How can I be sure that I am following through?

❷ Who can hold me to my commitment?

Write down the answers next to your actions.

Doing It. Now go. You know what to do. You know when to do it. By taking action today or this week, you are officially creating your new life! Hooray!

As you move forward, *keep* making commitments and taking action until you create the life you want to bring your baby into! We encourage you to keep building your action plan and adding more items from your prioritized list, including the things you want to let go. Remember, you can use the exercise in "A Closer Look" to create a special action plan suited to your style.

For inspiration or motivation, turn back to the notes you've collected as you've gone through this book. Review your worksheets in the "Keepsakes" section, flip back through your journal, or revisit your notes to reconnect with your vision for your ideal first year. You have compelling reasons to take action. Stay connected to your vision, your values, and your commitment to yourself, baby, and family.

KEEPSAKE

Fill out "My Action Plan" in the "Keepsakes" section in Appendix A or in your own journal or notebook.

TIPS FOR TAKING ACTION

- Spend more time taking action than making the plan.
- Communicate your commitments!
- Find someone to encourage you and hold you accountable.

Common Experiences _____

These last steps in the process are exciting and rewarding. Finally, you're actually making things happen! Taking concrete steps toward the life you've envisioned makes becoming a mother so *real*. Here is what some mothers-to-be found as they took action.

Tackling Big Changes. Makala was a woman who was pretty frightened when she first became pregnant. As much as she wanted the baby, she felt pressured by the financial implications. She also felt trapped. They had a big house with a big mortgage to match, and big jobs to be able to make that payment. In a moment of clarity, Makala realized that she didn't actually have to have any of it. As a result, she and her partner took a very bold step: They decided to downscale. They began to make plans to move to a smaller house and the pressure began to ease. "I'm letting go of my old idea of who I am," Makala declared as she prepared for the move. "My baby will never remember we lived in a smaller house. But she will remember that I was less anxious and was able to spend more time with her." It all started when she boldly chose to "break free from our financial handcuffs"—her biggest, most terrifying catalyst—as the place to start taking action. Sometimes tackling the biggest challenges first makes everything else come together. Don't be afraid to start big.

Starting Small. Ana took the opposite approach and began checking off the smaller items on her list. Geared up and ready to make changes, she wanted to jump in with action steps she could take right away—and her catalysts seemed too intimidating. One of her first steps was to put in place a nice-to-have: She bought herself a great pair of glasses. "I only wear contacts and never wear glasses because I had this old pair from ten years ago. But, I knew that I couldn't be putting in my contacts at two o'clock in the morning, so I bought really cool glasses! It felt so powerful! I thought, 'Look—I changed that!'" Taking little steps like Ana did can get the momentum going and lay the groundwork for making more and even bigger changes.

Judging Yourself. When you look at your prioritized list, parts of it may seem silly or strange. But if it's important to you, it's important to take action. Cynthia felt this way about her dog, Max. Secretly, she cared just as much about how her dog would fare in the first year as she did about the new baby! She almost crossed "prepare Max" off her prioritized list, but the truth was, Max meant the world to her. Doing her best to shut out imagined judgments ("It's just a dog; don't be silly"), she got online and searched for "dog and new baby." She found several helpful books on the subject and ordered one that very same day. Instead of judging herself, she simply took action. This step eased her fears, and Cynthia learned a lot about how to bring a baby into a home with a dog. As you go through your list and take action, be careful about allowing the perceived judgments of others to hold you back. Instead, commit to staying focused on what you want.

Finding Support. One of the most exciting parts of taking action is how consistently validating it is. Sure, some people may balk—those people who don't want you to change or aren't happy about the way the changes affect them. But for the most part, people are amazingly supportive when a woman has a baby. It is one of those unifying events that can bring out the soft spot in anyone. So the brutal boss who usually cracks the whip suddenly backs off when you need a break, and your friends don't try to talk you into a latte when you've cut out caffeine. As you communicate the action steps you're taking, listen to the positive feedback. The support can encourage you even more.

On Your Way

You're doing it! By making commitments and taking action, you are no longer designing your life for the future; you are living it. When you start to take action, your life will begin to change with its own momentum. Taking action on your catalysts and what is most important really does work. Working on the nice-to-haves is good, but when you stay focused on what matters most to you, your new life will take off.

We know that these actions take discipline and focus. It *is* a commitment. But remember: If you have followed this process, every action you take will reflect your true values, beliefs, and intention. As a result, what you are doing is literally propelling your *new life* into being, just as you are bringing a *new being* into life.

 How am I moving forward?

C O N G R A T U L A T I O N S !

You have launched your new life! We want to acknowledge you for

- Picking a place to start.
- Taking specific action.
- Creating momentum.
- Starting to live your ideal life today.

A Closer Look

Exercise: Personalizing Your Action Plan

Before you jump into making your action plan, we have some suggestions. In our coaching, we have seen people lose steam as soon as it comes time to take action; a poor action plan is one of the reasons. To solve this problem, use the ideas below to create a customized action plan that is compelling to you.

- **Understanding the elements of an action plan.** However you design your action plan, it should have these characteristics.

1. It states what you want to achieve (your catalysts or other items).
2. It shows which actions to do and when to do them.
3. It clearly gives you a way to choose what to do next.
4. It enables you to track your progress.
5. It motivates you and draws you back again and again to ask, what's the next action I can take?

- **Knowing yourself.** If you want a plan that will spur you on, it's best to know what kinds of things motivate you to take action. This way you can personalize your plan to be uniquely suited to your way of thinking and doing.

If you're an analytical type who loves charts, lists, and tables, your action plan might look similar to our "Sample Action Plan" in this section. But if this is the kind of plan that you would shove in a drawer, you might need something more creative and outside-the box. Here are some questions to ask to get you thinking about what might work best for you:

❓ How do I think? (Linearly, logically, hierarchically? Or more laterally, circular, or maybe weblike?)

❓ What helps me understand? (Is it colors, images, charts, graphs, words, diagrams, pictures, objects?)

EXTRA RESOURCES

An electronic version of the action plan worksheet is available at **www.empoweredmotherhood.com.**

❓ What motivates me? (Checking things off? Getting a gold star? Seeing a pile get smaller?)

• **Choosing your approach.** Now take what you learned about yourself and the elements that you need in an action plan and create your own approach! Consider all of the innovative ways you could create an action plan that go beyond the old standard of a bulleted list. Feel free to use one of the following brilliant ways we have seen moms-to-be take on this task.

A Map: Draw a map of the territory you're covering. It might depict the things you want as symbols or pictures, with action items as stepping stones along the road that leads from where you are now to where you want to be. Stick in pins to show how far you have come.

A Big Poster: On poster paper create a giant diagram that graphically details your action plan using shapes, arrows, boxes, lines, and words. Use fun stickers to denote finished tasks.

Grab Bag: Write your catalyst/item and the associated action items on small squares of paper. Fold them and put them in a bag or jar. Each day, draw one out and ask, "What am I going to do today?" When your bag is empty, you're done or it's time to add more actions!

A Post-It Wall: You can write action items on sticky notes and post them all over a wall. Each time you complete an action, you get to rip one off. You're done when your wall is clean!

A Picture or Mural: You can draw a mural showing what you want to do visually, labeling your action with captions below. Not feeling artistic? You can also use pictures from magazines to get the same effect.

And don't get so caught up in making your action plan that you forget to take action. Remember, your action plan is meant to be a prompt, not a distraction.

• **Taking action.** No matter what shape your action plan takes, now is the time to use it. Dive in and start taking action—it's the most important step of this process.

Be sure to add anything you want to "My Action Plan" in the "Keepsakes" section in Appendix A or put your action plan where you will revisit it every day!

Sample Action Plan

Catalyst/Important/ Nice-to-Have	Action	When	Who	Done
Help around the house	Make a list of everything we need done (laundry, cleaning, meals, etc.)	By June 1	Me	
	Ask around for teenagers to do odd jobs and babysitting	By June 30	Andy	
	Figure out how much money we could spend on hiring some help	By June 15	Me	
Room for the baby	Look online for space-savers	Sat. a.m.	Me	
	Measure front and back rooms; decide if we want to rearrange	Tonight	Me & Andy	
	Talk to friends (Ann, Sylvie . . . ?) about having a baby sleep in our room vs. their own room	Ask at Bunko	Me	
	Make a list of what we'll need; what's a "need" and what's a "want"?	By July 31	Me & Andy	
Confidence!!!	Talk to Beth about Mom's "telling me how to do it" issue (Ask her how she handled it when Aaron was born)	Call her tomorrow (Fri.) - go to lunch	Me Beth	
	*Ask Beth to hold me accountable!			
	Buy two or three books on babies and parenting (Does Cindy have any I can borrow? Any good suggestions?)	By May 20	Me Cindy	
	Call Ginny's counselor?	Talk to Mom first	Me Mom	

Lessons in BECOMING A MOTHER

Lesson 9 **Asking for What You Want**

Boldly make requests and get what you need.

Now that it's time to actually get what you want for your life, you're going to need some help. For some women—lots of us, actually—it's hard to ask. The reasons range from martyrdom, to fear of appearing selfish, to lingering issues of self-worth, to avoidance of obligation. Whatever the reason, lack of expertise in making requests is a handicap when taking action for your new life. Here are a few key ideas to help you ask for what you want, whatever that may be.

Remembering to Ask

The first rule of asking for what you want is this: It's your job to ask. It's their job to say yes or no. The idea is self-explanatory, but it is amazing how these roles tend to cross. Let's take a closer look.

First, it's your job to ask. It is *not* your job to imply, hope, or expect the other person to intuit what you need. It is also not your job to answer. That means you don't get to deny the other person the chance to help you or answer for them. You don't even get to guess what his or her answer will be. Your only job is to ask. Just focus on that.

Second, it's the other person's job to say yes or no. Both answers are perfectly all right. Accept them both in advance. If the answer is no, you're going to ask somebody else or find another creative way of getting your needs met. But the chances are the person will probably say yes and be glad you asked. Note, too, that it is *not* someone else's job to discover what you need. If you're expecting anyone to do your job by asking you what *you* need, you're expecting too much.

It's your job to ask. It's the other person's job to say yes or no.

Setting the Terms

The beauty of asking for what you want is that you can ask for it how, when, and of whom you like. You do this by setting the terms.

Decide *exactly* what it is you want. Be specific. What day? What time? Who do you want to ask? For example, let's say you want to go to your book club, which meets on Tuesday nights at six o'clock, as a way of staying in touch with friends. You ask for *that*. Rather than vaguely mentioning to a friend, "I'd love to go to book club if I can" (hoping she'll take the hint and offer to babysit), instead you purposely call that friend with this request and ask her to come over Tuesday at six.

Be specific. Assume people want to give you exactly what you need, and go ahead with your request. Don't be surprised if this works so well you want to do it again.

Being Ready to Receive

Unless you surround yourself with a gang of selfish ogres, we can almost promise you'll get a positive response to many of your requests. The reason? *People love to help expectant women and new mothers.* There are probably a lot of people in your life who find enjoyment, meaning, and purpose in helping other people. Since it's someone they love who's asking—that's you—they will most likely be delighted you asked, agree readily to help you, and possibly give you more than you asked for.

Allow this time to be your chance to receive, knowing that your time to be a giver will come again. Let other people have the joy of giving to you. The only way you can do that is if you offer them the chance. Now is the time to secure the things you think you're going to want after the baby is born. Why not ask? Soon you will have gathered a group of close friends and family who will *all* be willing to help.

CHAPTER TEN

Step 10
CELEBRATING YOUR NEW LIFE

"So many of our dreams at first seem impossible,
then they seem improbable, and finally,
when we summon the will, they become inevitable."
—*Christopher Reeve*

Take a good look at yourself. You have arrived! You have moved from a woman dreaming about new motherhood to a woman truly *living* her new life. By completing this process, you have made a generous investment in your future and the future of your family. We hope that as you continue to put your plan into action that you will feel both proud and excited about what's to come! You have immense inner wisdom and ability to create your life. And you will continue using those gifts as you move into the life you've been anticipating all this time.

In this chapter, you get to savor your accomplishments. You give yourself permission to sit back and relish the results of your efforts and celebrate what you have created in this process! Before your baby even arrives, you get to embrace your *own* arrival as the new you who is ready to be a mother.

Don't Miss the Celebration!

In this last step of the process you will celebrate everything you have done in the past weeks and who you have become. This celebration will help you integrate your experience as well as recognize your own growth. You get to reflect on what you are proud of and all that you have accomplished. This kind of celebrating fortifies your commitment and advances your growth in a way that will be especially rewarding when your baby is here. Let loose and just relax. You are amazing!

At this stage in the process it's easy to *stop*. You've envisioned what you want, you've created a plan, and you're putting that plan into action. What else is there? After all, you're on your way! But without celebration, all that effort can feel empty— as though you've just checked off another task on your list. Creating your life is so much more than that. Celebration isn't just a way of acknowledging that you reached the goal or the end of the process, it's recognizing who you have become. In many ways *this is the real reward.*

When you started this book, you probably wanted to *feel* a certain way. In addition to wanting to arrange your time and the physical aspects of your life to make room for a baby, you wanted to feel something—maybe in control, maybe at peace, or maybe happy. Celebrating at the end of the process is the way to connect with that feeling, so that you're not just *doing* what you wanted to do, but *being* who you wanted to be.

> *"Reading these chapters has been such a journey for me! The writing has been a companion to me through a new spurt of growth and consciousness. I look at celebration as a destination: My journey is constantly a focus for me, which is good. But I need rest stops too, to contemplate the view, to breathe and be aware of the distance traveled. And to carry that joy into further travel."*   —EMMA, 9 MONTHS PREGNANT

Your celebration isn't an event. It is enjoying a new outlook on life. It's learning how to be connected to the present you've created and realizing that you have done something tremendous…and loving every moment of it.

> *"I always forget this part! I tell myself that I take time to high five myself and I never do. Maybe I get superstitious or something, like don't jinx it by pointing out that something has gone well. Thanks for making me relax into a moment of celebration."*   —MARY, 8 MONTHS PREGNANT

FINDING YOUR OWN WAY
Celebrate!

Now you get to celebrate! You certainly deserve to do so. Take time to acknowledge your efforts and choose the most appealing way to celebrate your accomplishment. Don't forget to include your husband or partner and anyone else who has been part of your process.

Acknowledging Yourself. Set aside time for this last step. The whole point of celebrating is to stop and mark the occasion, and you can't do that if you're constantly on the move! Give yourself space to reflect. This moment is about you. It's about noticing what you have done and what you have created—heightening your awareness instead of rushing past it. Stop, reflect, and thoughtfully acknowledge yourself.

Think back to the beginning of the book and reflect on the following questions:

- How am I different now than when I started?
- How is my life different?
- Do I have the same fears? Which ones have I overcome?
- How have I started to honor my values and beliefs on a daily basis?
- Am I closer to who I intend to be?
- What gifts did the process bring?
- Where did I push past my own comfort zone?
- What significant steps have I taken?
- What can I now give my baby?

Notice how it feels to acknowledge yourself in this way. See how exceptional you are. People live lives every day in which their dreams go unspoken, to say nothing of unlived. You have taken a stand for your life, your baby, and your family! You have gone through a process—an intense and rigorous process—to define, design, and begin to create your ideal life, and that is something to celebrate. Sing your own praises. Stand up right now and acknowledge yourself out loud:

I am proud of myself for . . .

I surprised myself by . . .

I am so happy and grateful that . . .

Marking the Occasion. Decide who you most want to celebrate with and throw your own little commemoration event. This might be as simple as a phone call or a lovely dinner, or you might decide you'd like to throw a real party!

There are as many ways to celebrate your accomplishments as you can think up. Here are a few of our favorite celebrations from women we've known:

- Take a photo. For the next eighteen years, and probably more, photographs take on a new importance as you capture your baby in every one of his or her precious milestones. This is *your* precious milestone. Take a picture of yourself in all your pregnant beauty as a reminder of this special time or of something else that will evoke this moment. Like Susan—she took a snapshot of the gorgeous Atlantic shore where she did most of her journaling throughout this process. Framed in her living room, it looks to others like a scenic view; to her it is a celebration of her creation.

- Take a vacation. Keva took a real vacation with her husband to a mountain resort. But vacations can also be simple—like a two-hour retreat to the spa or even a quiet day off at home. Spending time with yourself is one way to celebrate life, or you can invite other people to join.

- Steal away for a romantic night for two. Marleen took her partner to their favorite Italian restaurant, and they toasted their commitment to a spectacular first year.

- Have a girls' night. Romance is great, but sometimes there's nothing like sharing the joys of life with your girlfriends. Julie had a dessert night with her three best friends who had supported her through her various moments of panic and preparation.

- Take yourself shopping! Buy yourself something special that will signify putting yourself first, that makes you feel fabulous, and that will go with you into the new phase of your life. Gail bought a bracelet with a fertility symbol charm. Whitney purchased a fine pen and journal, and Rosalind bought a pear tree and planted it in the backyard.

Spreading the Word. You are becoming a mother who will *not* lose herself, but many women still do. In the opening letter to this book, we shared our mission to rewrite the stories of new motherhood for our generation—to help women escape the impossible choices that sometimes present themselves along with a new baby. One way of celebrating your arrival is to invite another mother to follow your path. You can do this by describing what you've learned and sharing this book with other moms-to-be so that they, too, will make this time of their lives as special and empowering as you have.

Commemorating the Moment. There is one final ritual. Many expectant mothers choose to write a letter to themselves to open on their baby's first birthday. This is a meaningful and joyful way to conclude your work.

The benefit of a letter is to see yourself fully living the life of your dreams. You and your new life may not always reflect your ideal. By confirming your vision in writing, you make it easier to move forward—like knowing your destination before you strike out on a journey. Writing the letter puts you deeply in that space of who and where you want to be, and what you want for your life, one more time. Suggestions for writing the letter and a sample from one of our mothers-to-be are in "A Closer Look" at the end of the chapter.

KEEPSAKE

Record your ideas for celebrating in "My Celebration" in the "Keepsakes" section of Appendix A—then go out and celebrate!

TIPS FOR CELEBRATING

- Do something! Don't skip this step.
- Connect your celebrating with the most meaningful aspect of your process.
- Treat yourself like you would treat your best friend.

Common Experiences

Celebrating should be easy! There are no more decisions to make, no hard actions to take, no major challenges to get through. Celebrating is one of the most rewarding steps you can take to fully realize your new life. Yet celebrating is so much more than the final step in the process. In many ways, it is a new beginning. Here are some ways other expecting mothers experienced their celebration.

Skipping This Step. Perhaps the most common tendency is to skip the celebration altogether. Even if you feel you're still in the middle of the process or feel ready to move on to other things, permit yourself to stop and commemorate this moment. What would life be if we didn't celebrate? How would it feel to have no birthdays, no holidays, no parties? When you look back over the years of your life, is it not the celebrations that make life magical?

Chris is one mother-to-be who had to be gently pulled back into celebration. Excited about her plans to move forward and deeply engaged in the process of eliminating her obstacles, she was eager to learn more, ask questions, and keep going. Certainly, we wanted her to do that! But, it was also important for her to see how far she had come. Chris had shifted from an almost resigned perspective of accepting that she would have to give up big parts of her life by having a baby to a woman running onto the field of her life, flags flying. When Chris could slow down long enough to look back at this image of herself, rushing gleefully into motherhood with all of her natural exuberance, a smile burst onto her face. Modestly, she admitted, "I guess it is pretty neat."

Seeing Yourself Through New Eyes. Even before the baby is born, many women start to see themselves differently. Celebrating gives your mind a chance to catch up with your life; to realize that you *have* broken through to new possibilities.

Shauna was surprised to see herself as someone who had dreamed her way into change. A very practical, grounded woman, she had initially resisted envisioning her life and was much more interested in knowing "what to do." By the time she had finished the process, she realized that it was her original visualization that led her to where she ended up. Shauna saw that she had more creativity than she thought—and more importantly, she learned that creativity could be her guide.

Mel, on the other hand, saw herself as a woman who had "stepped into her light." She realized that in the past she had taken a back seat in her life. Abdicating most of the decisions to her husband, she was unaccustomed to steering. Designing her life for new motherhood not only got Mel to steer, it also showed her that she could be bold enough to go where *she* wanted to go. Moreover, she learned that her husband supported her in her growth and development. The end result was a deeper relationship built on trust and collaboration.

Chances are you have experienced some changes by preparing to become a mother in such a thoughtful way as you have done through our process. Celebrating helps you get to know the new you. Taking a moment to celebrate may help you see how far you've really come.

Feeling Shy About Expressing Your Joy. As much as we celebrate as a culture, we women don't always celebrate *ourselves*. Maybe that's why it will be your best friends who throw you a baby shower, not yourself. It may feel uncomfortable, even vain, to be the one to showcase your own arrival at the end of this process. The word "self-congratulatory" has a negative connotation; we want you to redefine it for yourself. Adopt self-congratulations as a meaningful step in acknowledging how you've grown.

Feeling Transformed. Many of the women we coach going through the process of *Becoming a Mother* experience an emotional transformation that has them feeling ready for motherhood. Jan noticed that she had become more confident, more creative, and more determined since she started *Becoming a Mother*. Several of her friends had commented on how positive she seemed, saying that it must be because she was pregnant. Jan didn't agree that it was just the hormones that were making her glow; she actually did feel more joyful. Lucy felt closer to her partner. Pat felt empowered and bold. Ginny felt peaceful. Above all, expecting mothers finish this process feeling exhilarated!

Feeling Grateful. When you notice what you've done to prepare for your baby, there's a good chance you'll suddenly feel grateful. As Eleanor put it, "At the end of the process, I had a moment of deep gratitude, for everything incredible and marvelous that is my life *today*. I've been so focused on the baby coming—the miracle of birth, that when I stopped, I really noticed the miracle of my life right now."

The Birth of Your New Life

Throughout this book, we have acknowledged that no matter how you plan, life sometimes takes twists and turns that you don't expect. But how you handle those twists and turns depends entirely upon your perspective and preparation. You now have both.

You have a perspective on new motherhood that is empowering and confident. You know that you have the ability to create the kind of life you want: one in which your baby is received by the most healthy, confident mother he or she could hope for. You know what values, beliefs, and intention you want to honor. You have a new perspective on motherhood that you *can* be a mother without losing yourself.

And you are prepared. You have a whole set of skills that you can use any time you like to recreate your life again and again, until it is absolutely what you want it to be. Every exercise you did in this process will stay with you. What you have learned may whisper wisdom in your ear when you need it most or pop up as a brilliant idea when you're looking for an answer. Lots of things will change after you give birth. Your values might shift again or become refined after your baby arrives. They may shift again after the first year or the fifth. But the foundation and the process you've gone through to honor yourself will be yours forever.

You are a woman with initiative, creativity, resourcefulness, and commitment. You have completed this process out of love for your baby and a strong desire to feel fulfilled and at peace in your life. We wish you all the returns you have earned—an exuberant sense of joy in life, the satisfaction of knowing *you* get to create your life, and finally, the grateful, unconditional love of your baby. We wish you well.

 What am I savoring at this moment?

CONGRATULATIONS!

You are completing a thoughtful journey into new motherhood. We want to acknowledge you for

- Recognizing how far you've come.
- Taking the time to slow down and celebrate.
- Finding lasting ways to keep the feeling alive.
- Becoming a mother without losing yourself!

A Closer Look

Exercise: A Letter to Myself on My Baby's First Birthday

Your task is to write a letter to *you*—the "you" who will celebrate your baby's first birthday. This is a chance to capture the essence of your new life by describing what has happened in the first year. Below are ideas of what you can write about, but we encourage you to write this letter *your* way.

Imagine yourself on the day of your baby's first birthday. Who are you now, who have you been? And who do you want to be for your baby on this day? Write about the qualities you will have developed a year after your baby's birth. Write what you love about this future self of yours and what you are proud of.

Describe the life you imagine, one year out, and notice how much you're enjoying it. What has changed for you? What is life like for you as a mother? As a woman? Where will you be financially, socially, and professionally? What have you created for your baby?

Write about how you honored your values, beliefs, and intention, about the actions you will have taken, and the obstacles you've overcome. The letter can recognize everything this process has brought to your life and your family.

Don't forget to save your letter! Put it in a safe place that you will remember. Put a note in your calendar to remind you to read it again on your baby's first birthday. You'll be surprised how much of the letter will ring true! You may also want to revisit your letter before then to keep you close to your dreams.

EXTRA RESOURCES

Go to **www.empoweredmotherhood.com** for a special digital recording of us that will enhance your celebration!

Sample:

A Letter to Myself on My Baby's First Birthday

Dear Wendy,

What a joy it is to see where you are now! Congratulations! I know it's been a year of miracles, a year of arrival, and a year of unfolding dreams.

Here are the things I'm proud of you for. I'm most of all proud of you for becoming more open. You are far more flexible and curious about trying new ways and flowing with the changes in your life. You are peaceful in your approach to every day. It comes across as a calm, loving confidence, and it becomes you.

Remember last January when your friend accused you of moving so fast that you weren't "experiencing life fully"? You took that to heart. You've started saying "no" more often. You've delegated tasks to other people who can do them well, and you've let go of them. You've referred clients and opportunities to other people who will benefit from them greatly, so that you can focus on doing the few things that matter most and that you do exceptionally well. You've made it a policy not to do things you don't really want to do and don't have time for.

You have learned so much in all of the areas of your life. Money—your new system of customer referrals has created a steady cash flow, leaving you more trusting and relaxed. Your new attitude toward spending and Hugh's successful career shift are moving you toward the financial freedom you seek! Family and friends—your community is so loving and supportive. Their help in the first few months, especially around your afternoon catnaps, was incredible. The baby has brought everyone together in surprising ways. You see good friends often, and you've made a lot of new friends who have babies the same age as yours. Health—a regular workout routine is back, and so is your figure! You really gave your body time to naturally recover from the birth and early motherhood. Learning—your three-month maternity leave was the best gift you ever gave yourself. The time to just be with your baby and learn who he is with no pushing or rushing made it a very special time. You had so much fun exploring the baby development books, discovering new things about yourself, and using skills you never dreamed you had. Your growth as a mother has spilled over into all areas of your life.

And finally, the best for last! Our close-knit little family circle is more than I could have hoped for. You, Mama, have stepped into motherhood gracefully and with confidence. You were a natural from the beginning. You must have known that you would be good at this! And you are. As a result, your baby is deeply loved and cared for by two amazing parents who confidently and intuitively create the structure that he needs. He is full of laughter and wonder, inspiring the same in you and Hugh. It's the best of all possible worlds for him and his well-adjusted parents.

With love and anticipation,

Me!

Lessons in BECOMING A MOTHER

Lesson 10 **Savoring Every Moment**

Be present in and relish every moment.

Savoring is all about deepening your awareness of the present and drinking in the experience. There's so much to savor when you're expecting a baby—the feeling of anticipation, the excitement, the happiness of the way your life is now, to say nothing of everything that's about to come. Take the time to enjoy this moment. And when your baby brings a host of new opportunities to savor life, you will be glad you've learned how to be present. You won't miss a thing.

Relishing the Moment

What do you love about your life? Don't just answer the question, find those things and enjoy them, right now in this moment. When you do, life takes on a deeper level of meaning and value.

To savor life as it takes place, you have to be *present*. Being present means tuning into and noticing what's happening around you. Watch and listen with your whole heart open, breathing in the experience with all of your senses. A fleeting peal of laughter when your husband makes a joke, a glance around the table when you have friends over for dinner, a particularly satisfying feeling when your boss commends your work. Life is made up of these moments. Pay attention and notice the details that make life rich.

Indulge yourself in the luxury of this very minute—wherever you are. For example, you might savor your naps while you are still pregnant. Notice the couch or bed beneath you, feel how it supports you. Burrow under the blanket and notice its texture and weight. Stretch your body—see where you feel loose or tight. Run your hands over your belly. Hear yourself breathe. Delight in the delicious feeling of sleep and space to dream. Savoring by soaking up the moment allows you to deepen the quality of your life.

Taking Snapshots

Savoring is like taking snapshots of moments in time. Instead of hanging a photo on the wall, you can save the image in your heart. To do this, all you have to do is slow down. Again—be present, notice the details, relish the experience, and then commit to remembering it. Close your eyes and memorize the moment, imprinting the image in your mind. Your private snapshots let you carry your memories with you in a special and lasting way.

This is the time to SAVOR! Every end is a beginning, and every beginning is an end. As you make the transition into becoming a mother, take the time to savor every moment.

CLOSING THOUGHTS

As we think about you now—on this incredible journey into motherhood—we are moved by your commitment to yourself. You are brilliant, you are brave, and you are setting an example for other mothers-to-be.

Becoming a mother will stretch you in new ways—ways we can't describe because you have to experience them yourself.

We don't know if *Becoming a Mother* has prepared you for those first few weeks with your baby, when everything is new and incredibly challenging. You might cry a lot. (We did.) You might lose confidence. (We all do.) You might wonder what Mother Nature was thinking when she entrusted you with a baby.

What we do know is that if motherhood knocks you off your feet, you have everything you need to pull yourself up. You will show up for your baby in the best possible way. As it gets easier and your new life takes shape, you will find more strength inside yourself than you ever imagined. Your resourcefulness, courage, and creativity give you almost everything you need to figure out life as a mother. Your love will fill in the gaps.

We are hoping that this book and everything it contains will be useful right now, after your baby is born, and for the rest of your life. As one new mother put it, "Use your foundation for motherhood as a compass. When the baby arrives and your new life really begins, you can adjust your direction as necessary." Make sure to keep the notes from your process handy and take them out after the baby arrives. They will remind you of what's important to you and what you need to feel fulfilled as a woman and mother.

You're ready. Welcome to motherhood.

Joelle and Amy
Mother's Day, 2006
Share your experience of becoming a mother, write to us at stories@empoweredmotherhood.com.

KEEPSAKES

A Record for *Becoming a Mother*

Throughout the process of *Becoming a Mother,* you are thinking, writing, and dreaming in ways that will guide you into your new life. We offer this space to record your ideas. You may want to refer to these pages from time to time as you take further steps in your transition into motherhood. You may also enjoy returning to them in the future as a special reminder of what it meant for you to become a mother. Electronic versions of all the *Becoming a Mother* worksheets are available at www.empoweredmotherhood.com so that you can use them again and again.

My Exploration

My Vision

My Foundation for Motherhood

Values

1. Value: _____

_____

2. Value: _____

_____

3. Value: _____

_____

4. Value: _____

_____

5. Value: _____

_____

6. Value: _____

_____

7. Value: _____

_____

Beliefs

-
-
-
-
-

Intention:

My Prioritized List

Catalysts

-
-
-
-
-

Important

-
-
-
-
-

Nice to Have

-
-
-
-

I Let Go of

-
-
-
-
-

My Models

My Ideal Year

Month:	Month:	Month:
Milestones:	Milestones:	Milestones:
Month:	Month:	Month:
Milestones:	Milestones:	Milestones:
Month:	Month:	Month:
Milestones:	Milestones:	Milestones:
Month:	Month:	Month:
Milestones:	Milestones:	Milestones:

My Ideal Month

Sunday					
Monday					
Tuesday					
Wednesday					
Thursday					
Friday					
Saturday					

My Ideal Week

	Notes
Sunday	
Monday	
Tuesday	
Wednesday	
Thursday	
Friday	
Saturday	

My Ideal Day

6:00 _____   **3:00** _____

7:00 _____   **4:00** _____

8:00 _____   **5:00** _____

9:00 _____   **6:00** _____

10:00 _____   **7:00** _____

11:00 _____   **8:00** _____

12:00 _____   **9:00** _____

1:00 _____   **10:00** _____

2:00 _____   [add other hours as needed]

My Ideal Budget

My Ideal Home

My Parking Lot

Questions	Things That Seem Impossible	Obstacles

My Possibilities Chart

Challenge:

Possibilities:

Challenge:
Possibilities:

Challenge:

Possibilities:

My Action Plan

Catalyst/Important/ Nice-to-Have	Action	When	Who	Done

My Celebration

MOTHER'S HELPER

We have tried throughout this book *not* to give you advice and to help you find your own path and truth. But in our experience coaching new mothers, as well as with our own babies, we have learned a few tips worth passing on. They're not scientific, but they do help make those early days of motherhood just a little bit easier. We offer them to you here in hopes of giving your life as a mother a head start.

Although there are plenty of tips on taking care of your body and your baby that we could include, we are leaving that advice to the professionals—your OB, midwife, doula, lactation specialist, or pediatrician. The information and ideas we are sharing are of a general nature and designed for educational purposes only. If you have *any* concerns about your health or the health of your child, you should always consult with a physician or healthcare professional.

Also know that some of the tips will align with your values and some will not. We do not advocate any particular lifestyle or baby-rearing philosophy (e.g., cloth vs. disposable diapers, breastfeeding vs. formula, cribs vs. co-sleeping). Take what advice makes sense to you and fits in with how YOU want to be a mother and to lead your life. Leave the rest.

We are always expanding and improving Mother's Helper—check www.empoweredmotherhood.com for the latest version.

Know Your Priorities

1. Take care of your baby.

2. Sleep.

3. Take care of yourself.

Save everything else until you're ready.

Make Life Easy

When you have a baby, your body accomplishes one of the most remarkable physical feats known in the natural word: giving birth. It deserves a break, and so do you. Here are some of our favorite ideas for making life easy so you can rest and recover. (We suggest you share these with your husband or partner, getting everything lined up and ready before your baby is born!)

- **Paper plates and plastic ware**. Stock up on paper plates, paper napkins, plastic cups, and plastic ware before your baby is born. Even if it's just for a few days, you'll be relieved not to have to do any dishes. It's one less chore on your list.

- **Prepared meals.** Prepare frozen meals ahead of time and save them for when you're hungry but tired. Lasagne, casseroles, and burgers work great. More suggestions: Stock up on takeout menus (particularly for restaurants that deliver!), and fill the pantry so you can make easy meals (pasta, tuna sandwiches, soups). And of course, say "Yes!" to anyone who wants to bring you food.

- **Easy cleanups**. Take advantage of those popup cleansing wipes for the bathroom and kitchen. It will be quite some time before you can do a good scrub job, and these wipes will keep things clean and disinfected.

- **Sudsy water.** Keep a small plastic bucket (or the washer) filled with soapy water. Then you can just dump soiled baby clothes in as soon as you remove them. It cuts down on extra scrubbing, stain removers, and sorting the laundry.

- **Clothespins.** Tiny socks and two-piece outfits have a way of getting separated in the wash! Attach matching sets to each other with clothespins before you even put them in the laundry basket and save yourself a step or two in the process.

- **Layered sheets.** Changing sheets on a crib is a nightmare—especially in the middle of the night! Try keeping two sets of sheets on the crib mattress (mattress cover, clean sheet, another mattress cover, another clean sheet) to simplify the task of cleaning up after naptime and nighttime messes. If you need to make a sudden change, you just have to strip one set off and there's a clean set underneath. (Make sure the mattress covers are waterproof!)

Find a Routine for Yourself

Many books will advise you to put your babies on routines—sometimes strict and sometimes flexible—to help them get used to the rhythms of life. While you might or might not want a routine for your baby, we do suggest a routine for yourself. Especially in the first several weeks with a baby, it can feel like your life is in upheaval. Find out what helps you keep your sanity every day, and use that routine as a guide.

- **Patterns.** Some mothers find it easiest to set up a cycle they can repeat over and over throughout the day. For instance, here's Mandy's:
  - Feed Reagan
  - Play with Reagan
  - Feed myself
  - Do something productive—no matter how small!
  - Take a nap when Reagan takes a nap
- **Must-haves.** Other mothers focus on the three to five things they want to have happen every day. These were Jana's:
  1. Take a shower
  2. Go for a walk
  3. Talk to *someone* outside my house (my mom, a friend, a neighbor)
- **A simple schedule.** Setting daily milestones is another way to get some predictability into your day without losing that all-important flexibility. For example, this was Alex's:

6:00	Wake up and read the paper before Jordan wakes up
10:00	Walk with Sam and Isabelle
12:00	Lunch
3:00	Nap
5:00	Start dinner

A routine can help you be flexible and forgiving with yourself as a new mother while also taking your baby's needs (and your body's needs) into account. Best of all, it can help you gain a general sense of balance and control.

Keep a List

One of the things that makes some new mothers crazy is the sudden downshift into a very slow pace. Your early days with your baby are busy, yet you still seem to get nothing done! Your time goes into feeding, diapering, bathing, holding, and learning about your baby, and before you know it, another day has gone by. A good system of keeping lists can be a lifesaver. Even if you're not getting things done, your list allows you to achieve peace of mind.

Here are some helpful suggestions for making a list work with a new baby.

1. **Prioritize.** You may have found it helpful in making your prioritized list to use our system of catalysts, important items, nice-to-haves, and things to let go. The same system works well in your everyday life.

2. **Do it your way.** In making your action plan, we suggested you find fun and creative approaches to collecting your ideas. Do the same for your list. Keep track of the things that need to get done—paying bills, picking up supplies, buying frames for all those new baby photos—in a way that makes sense to you and doesn't weigh you down.

3. **Let it go.** Go back to the first suggestion in this Appendix. Take care of your baby. Sleep. Take care of yourself. Pretty much everything else can go . . . at least for a while.

Be Prepared

One of the stress factors of motherhood is the *unexpected*. Anticipating what might happen can help you roll with the punches.

- **A stash of essentials.** There are plenty of things to stock up on before your baby comes to avoid those endless trips to the store. Think ahead for those things that spell disaster if you suddenly run out. A few key items to remember:
  - Menstrual pads (for the first few weeks of healing)
  - Medicated hemorrhoid pads (ditto)
  - Breast pads
  - Breast milk storage bags
  - Formula
  - Lanolin nipple cream
  - Diapers
  - Wipes

- **Extras to go.** Exploding diapers and excessive spitting up don't have to ruin your day. Keep a bag with an extra baby outfit, wipes, and diapers in the trunk of your car in the event of a "blowout." Most importantly, don't forget to keep an extra shirt in that bag for YOU when all that muck ends up all over your clean clothes!

- **Multiple changing stations.** Life seems a little less hectic if you have everything you need right where you need it. Cut back on constant running from room to room by setting up changing stations throughout the house. Buy a couple of decorative baskets and put in a few diapers, wipes, diaper cream, burp cloths, and a small towel for a changing pad. Place one in your bedroom and one in the living room (or the room you use most).

- **All strapped in.** Install your car seat long before your baby is set to come home and practice using it. Make sure a trained professional correctly installs it. You don't need the added stress of fussing over car seats with a newborn in your arms.

Get Organized

Adding a little person to your life can throw even the most organized homes into confusion. Here are a few tips to stay on top of the changes.

- **Make master lists.** Before you have the baby, or shortly after, create master lists you can use over and over. It cuts down on time and ensures you don't miss anyone or anything. A few good ones to have on hand: one master email distribution list of friends and family to use for baby announcements, one master list of babysitters or helpers, one master checklist for the grocery store, and one master list of diaper bag contents so you always know what to pack.

- **Keep track of gifts.** When you open baby gifts, write what you receive on the back of each accompanying greeting card and keep the cards in a pile. Then, as you write the thank you notes, you can check them off or throw them out.

- **Leave the tags on.** In an effort to feel ready to go, it's tempting to take the tags off the baby's new clothes. This is one area where we say: resist. You may find the sizes are wrong, styles out of season, or that your baby simply outgrows them before you even get them out of the closet. Leave the tags on and tape the receipt to the tags. If it makes you feel more prepared to have a few outfits at the ready, choose a handful to wash and save the rest for later when you know the seasons and the sizes you need.

- **Sort by size.** Whether you're organizing new clothes for the baby to grow into or storing clothes he's suddenly grown out of, keep them grouped by their size (don't go by the size on the tag, they are notoriously inaccurate—hold the clothes up to each other to match similar sizes). Plastic storage bins and magic markers work great for the task. Keep only the size that currently fits in the drawers and store the rest. When your baby is ready to move up, just pull out the next box and you're ready to go.

- **Make room.** Babies grow out of clothes so quickly. Put a bag or box in the closet and toss in any outfit as soon as you discover it's too small.

LEAVE THE HOUSE!

In our experience, nothing moves you out of new mother moodiness than a change of scenery. Promise yourself that in the first few weeks you will get out of the house. Take a walk. Go out for coffee. Visit your mom. Take your baby shopping. Sit at the beach. It doesn't have to be a big deal—in fact, it shouldn't be. We'll warn you—you might not feel like doing this when your baby is new. Just trust us, and you'll be so glad you did. Here are a few suggestions for making it happen.

- **Give yourself plenty of time.** Until you get used to the car seat, the stroller, and all of your baby's paraphernalia, even a jaunt to the drugstore will be an event. Cut down on the stress by allowing yourself plenty of time to figure everything out.

- **Get over the need to impress.** Yes, it would be nice to look fresh and rested, ironed and pressed, clean and made up before seeing your friends. It would be great if your baby had on her cutest outfit and didn't cry in public. Get over it. In the first few weeks after having your baby, let yourself be in a state of disarray if that's what it takes to leave the house. You'll be pleasantly surprised when everyone tells you how beautiful you look anyway and starts cooing over your adorable baby no matter what she's wearing.

- **Scout the nooks.** It's much easier to get out and about if you know how to make a quick escape in an emergency! Scope out the places in town that have great spaces for feeding and changing a baby. Upscale department store fitting rooms are ideal. Baby stores sometimes have mothers' rooms and many public places have family-sized restrooms. The comfy chairs in the back of the bookstore, the corner park, and even the waiting room at a doctor's office all tend to be friendly, quiet, private, understanding, or all of the above.

- **Go it alone.** It's liberating to learn to leave your house with a baby, but it's positively luxurious to take off by yourself. Find a loving babysitter (other moms are perfect!) and take yourself to a movie, on a walk, to the spa, or just for a drive. Don't be surprised if this little break moves you to tears.

Get Ready for Feeding: Top Three Tips

We were shocked when we learned how much time feeding our babies took, as well as how much there was to learn. Here are our top three tips for being prepared.

1. **Have ample burp cloths**. Again, these can cost you plenty if you spend top dollar for top fashion. We suggest good old-fashioned flour sack kitchen towels or cloth diapers. They're soft, they're white (read: bleachable), and they're cheap.

2. **Let other people help.** We know many heroic mothers who wow us with their unfailing commitment to feeding their babies themselves. It's a time to bond, it's easy (once you learn), and it's fun. But you can't do it when you're out on a date with your husband or partner. Consider getting a good breast pump if you're nursing and teaching your baby at least to accept a bottle, or keep some formula and a bottle in the diaper bag at all times. If nothing else, being set up to get help with feeding gives you an alternative if you ever can't get to your hungry baby.

3. **Make it fun!** No matter how special feeding time might be, the sheer volume of it can make it lose its luster. We know one new mom who stashed her feeding chair with snacks, good books, and all of her *Becoming a Mother* keepsakes so she could use the time to restore herself as well as her baby. Other moms have made feeding time a great chance to escape into reruns, read baby magazines to learn more about parenting, or catch up on conversations on the phone or in person.

Get Ready for Feeding: Bottles and Formula

If you're thinking of bottlefeeding your baby, the options for bottles and formula are overwhelming. Simplify the process with these suggestions.

- **Browse the aisles.** Take some time to window-shop before your baby arrives. Get a sense of the different versions of formula, bottles, and nipples available. Consult your pediatrician, your friends, and your supermarket shelves so you'll have a sense of your options. Remember that the hospital will also have formula available and usually gives you a few free bottles.

- **Make your first choice.** Once you know what's out there, make your best guess at what items will work for you. Buy a few and have them at the ready for your baby.

- **Experiment.** Once your baby arrives, you can switch things up to match his preference. He may gobble down the formula and hate the bottle, or the bottle may be fine but the formula gives him gas. Work with your baby's doctor to find the right combination—just don't be afraid to make the switch.

Get Ready for Feeding: Breastfeeding

Many a mother has been baffled at how difficult breastfeeding can be—at least in the first couple of weeks. How can something so natural be so hard? Here are a few ideas to get you into the groove.

- **Gather your resources.** Breastfeeding doesn't always come easily. Find out if your hospital has a lactation consultant, get the scoop on a breastfeeding support group, find a good book or two, and practice your patience. The right resources and the right frame of mind help make nursing successful.

- **Jog your memory.** If you have a hard time remembering which side you nursed on last (if you don't nurse both in each sitting), place a special bracelet or even a hair scrunchie on the wrist of the side you're nursing to help you remember. Yes, sleep deprivation definitely affects your short-term memory!

- **Prime the pump.** Even if you plan to breastfeed exclusively, get a pump system and have it ready before your baby comes. It can be instrumental in getting the breastfeeding going, relieving the pressure when your milk comes in (ow!), and at least gives you the option to let someone else feed your baby if you get sick, tired, or delayed on an errand.

Pamper Yourself (or Let Others Do It for You)

Did you know in some cultures new mothers stay off their feet for months? You might not be able to get on that program, but the spirit of it can sometimes be enough. You know what makes you feel soothed, and if you don't, this is the perfect time to learn. We've said it before, and we'll say it again. You've accomplished a remarkable feat. Reward yourself with a little special treatment. A few ideas:

- Take a real bath.

- Get a massage (have someone come to your house!).

- Get a haircut, a manicure, or a pedicure.

- Indulge in your favorite creams and lotions.

- Ask someone to bring you a special dessert or treat.

Get the Gear

You won't be able to resist holding your baby *a lot* in the first few weeks (who are we kidding—the next eighteen years). But there are times you'll want to be hands free, even if it's just to blow your nose. The baby business is booming with contraptions to make this possible. Remember that some pieces of equipment (exersaucers, doorjam jumpers, backpacks, sitting-up strollers) are meant for older babies who can sit up. Here are some ones that will best suit your newborn.

- **A sling** keeps your baby close at heart.

- **A front pack** also keeps your baby front and center.

- **A Moses basket** is a light and portable way to have your baby sleep or play close by, wherever you are.

- **A wraparound nursing pillow** can make nursing ten times easier.

- **A playpen** serves as a movable crib.

- **A good stroller** gets you out and about while keeping your baby safe and secure.

It could cost a fortune to buy all of this new. Instead, ask around. Babies only use these for a few weeks. Parents keep them in their garages for years.

Lean on Your Friends and Family

Don't resist asking friends and family for relief time and help on whatever you need. Most people are thrilled to carve out time to help a new mom and to be with the baby. Take advantage of it now, and without apology, you'll have your chance to return the good karma some day to the next new mom.

- **Be specific**. If anyone asks what they can do for you, go ahead and ask them for exactly what you need. Tell them you need something specific like picking up some diapers, doing the dishes, taking out the garbage, or cutting up some fruits and vegetables for you to snack on.

- **Focus on the baby.** If you have a helper (father, grandmother, sister, etc.) have him or her do all the prep work (laundry, clean dishes, prepare bottles, change the baby) so all you have to do is nurse and sleep.

- **Stretch it out.** Plan ahead and make sure you don't use up all of your favors in the first few days after the birth. You need the help even more after a few weeks when the steady stream of gifts, flowers, and food slows down.

- **Distinguish between visitors and help**. Some women are either too starved for conversation or too polite to take a much-needed break when friends arrive to help. If they truly have offered to help, and if you're comfortable with it, give yourself permission to excuse yourself to take a nap or run an errand while your guest enjoys time with your baby. Otherwise your "help" can turn into a constant stream of houseguests.

Lean on Your Partner

Throughout this book, you have probably given some thought to the way you and your partner will both be involved in taking care of your baby. When a little one actually arrives, however, both women and men sometimes fall back into old habits and traditional roles. Here are a few reminders to help you share the responsibility.

- **Trust in your partner's capabilities.** Don't fall into the trap of being the only person who can take care of the baby. Your husband or partner is perfectly able to handle any of the parenting tasks—including feeding the baby with a bottle, whether it's filled with formula or breast milk.

- **Make it work for both of you.** Different couples have different needs. Work with your partner to figure out how to split the roles. Maybe your partner is in charge of bottlefeeding an entire weekend night so you can sleep, or maybe it's his job to get up to change diapers while you do all of the feeding. One mother we know took primary care of the baby while her husband took primary care of *her* by making meals, picking up the house, and running errands. There's no right or wrong way to arrange the lives in a household; what matters is that the arrangement works for everyone.

- **Let your partner in.** It isn't just the work that you're sharing; it's also the joy and the bonding. Some women who insist on going it alone in the care and nurturing of their babies end up leaving their husbands out. Before long, they become exhausted and wonder why their partners just "couldn't relate" when they became short fused. When both parents fully participate, mutual understanding and compassion increase dramatically.

Great Gifts

The gifts that come with babies can rival Santa's workshop! But you and your baby need more than clothes, rattles, and yet another blanket. Give some thought to the gifts you need that don't fit nicely on a registry and then let your friends and family in on the secret. Here are some great gifts that can start off your new life as a mother. If no one offers to give you these gifts . . . consider giving them to yourself.

- **Meals and groceries.** Ask your friends to bring food instead of gifts. This is the number one tip from new moms. A home-cooked meal is the best thing in the world when you don't have the time or energy to cook!

- **A clean house.** A gift certificate for housekeeping—even if it's only once or twice—can ease your life and make you feel great.

- **Babysitting.** If your family or friends really want to give you something special, it might be a nap or the chance to go out on a date. Ask for an hour or two of babysitting as a nice way to give yourself a break and return to mothering feeling renewed.

- **A hands-free headset.** You won't find a telephone headset on the baby registry, but it's a great way to stay in touch with friends while you're busy with your baby around the house.

Cut Costs

At times it can seem that your baby requires the addition of a whole new income! Pinching pennies here and there can relieve some of the pressure.

- **Reuse.** Don't throw away those plastic bags your newspapers come in. Put them in your diaper bag to use for those stinky diapers while you are out! Plastic baby food jars make great tiny containers for snacks later on. Empty diaper boxes are just the right size for storing clothes.

- **Make your own travel packs.** In your diaper bag, put a handful of wipes in a plastic bag. It's lighter than a bulky box of wipes and less expensive than those travel-sized packs. (Plus, you can put a dirty diaper in the baggie after you use the wipes.)

- **Find cheap labor.** Make friends with reliable college students who need free food, groceries, and a washing machine and make a trade: your home-made goods for an hour or two of baby-holding. If a young person doesn't come to mind, contact a local church/youth group leader for possible candidates. Another option is to contact local clubs such as 4-H or girl/boy scouts for someone who may need to complete community service jobs for his or her program.

- **Be creative.** Plastic bowls, measuring spoons, and interestingly shaped (but safe) utensils make great toys and keep babies entertained.

- **Use hand-me-downs.** There is nothing wrong with gratefully taking your friend's offer to give you her son's barely worn outfits, toys, and gear. You too will be passing them on some day.

Get Away, Get Creative, and Get Some Time for You

Almost every mom we know sings the praises of time just for YOU! We suggest finding childcare once a week to help you get away, but even if you can't, here are some creative ways to make time for you.

- **Hit the gym.** If you can't find someone to come to your house, go where childcare already exists. Gyms and health clubs are perfect. You can take the time to go to a class, run on the treadmill, sit in the hot tub or sauna, or take a long hot shower. Exercise is therapeutic, so you feel great and get a little break!

- **Nap in the car.** If you find it tough to nap at home with the baby and a babysitter in the house, take your nap on the run. One mother we know could be found asleep in her car in the café parking lot, with the seat dropped back, pillow and blanket. Later she'd pop in for a coffee and read a book. Delicious!

- **Listen to a good book.** As a new mother, you spend a lot of time thinking baby thoughts. It can be refreshing to stimulate your intellect with a good book written for adults. Audio books, in particular, are an excellent way to get some mental interaction while you're working around the house, walking your baby, or driving around running errands.

A Pleasant, Peaceful Space

The joys of motherhood are made even sweeter when you feel peaceful in a pleasant space. A few simple steps can create a restful environment.

- **Turn off the ringer**. Answer the calls from well-wishers when the time is right for you.

- **Turn on the voice mail.** If the phone does ring when you're not ready, let it go to voice mail. You don't have to answer the phone every time it rings.

- **Turn on the auto-responder**. If you worry about emails stacking up and feel pressured to return all those messages, set up an auto-responder to communicate that you'll be out of touch for awhile. You can even attach a photo of the baby—people will understand your need to get away!

- **Turn off the TV**. Everyone likes a good show to escape, but TV can actually drain your energy instead of restoring it. Try music instead to soothe you, energize you, sing you to sleep, or set a mood. You might even enjoy a little silence.

- **Communicate your limits.** If friends, family, co-workers, employers, and clients are asking for more than you're ready to give, say so. Your boundaries may change day to day. Keep people informed of what you can and can't do, then stick to it.

- **Let the chores go.** Release the feeling that "you have to" keep it all going in those first three months and just be with your baby. Dancing, chatting, making up songs, and snuggling on the sofa build the bond and the memories. Plus they're fun and they feel good. Enjoy!

- **Meditate.** Five minutes of clearing your mind can feel like a long afternoon nap. It's a great activity to pair with feeding your baby or rocking her to sleep.

Capture the Moment

It's absolutely certain that sometime in the first year you will look back and realize how short the first few months of your baby's life really were. Although almost every mother has fervent intentions to document the precious moments, it's not always easy to find the time. Here are a few tips to capturing the moments.

- **Keep it simple.** Stash a notebook by the bed or rocking chair and jot down the memories and moments as you think of them, use a tape recorder, or scribble baby milestones on your household calendar—you can put them in the baby book later (or not!).

- **Make it convenient.** Keep a camera handy. Put it on the kitchen counter or someplace where you can quickly grab it the next time your baby does "the cutest thing ever." Try buying a couple of disposable cameras to spread around, including one for your diaper bag.

- **Don't go overboard.** Write in the journal, create the lovely scrapbook, take lots of pictures BUT NOT at the expense of enjoying and being present with your baby.

Connect with Fellow Moms

As one new mother put it, "Join a mother's group ASAP!" Every mother we know raves about the incredible reassurance and learning that comes from being with others who are going through the same thing. So, whether it is meeting up with the moms from your childbirth class, a La Leche League or mothers' support group, a mommy & me yoga class, or just another mother on your block, reach out and connect.

- **Don't wait.** It's easy to put this off because leaving the house with the baby can seem daunting. However, it's the early weeks where you most need the support. Nothing is more comforting than sitting in a roomful of moms all with crying, feeding, gurgling, and pooping babies. You really get that you are not alone.

- **Share.** Go ahead and vent your frustration, let loose with all of your fears, and brag plenty about your little one and how amazing he is. This is the place where all of your emotions will be welcome and understood.

- **Listen up.** You often will get the best and most practical advice from other mothers who are dealing with the exact same challenges you are. Take advantage of the wisdom.

Nurture Your Relationship

Don't forget your marriage or relationship. It's amazing how quickly the vow you made to keep your relationship a top priority can start to crumble with lack of sleep, 24/7 responsibilities, and a new consuming love. Look for ways to keep your relationship strong and growing.

- **Don't include the baby.** Make a point to put the baby down and "snuggle" with HIM too. Even 15 minutes alone can work wonders.

- **Don't wait too long.** Some mothers postpone that first date night for two years or more! Do something with your significant other within two or three weeks of the baby's birth, even if just going out for an ice cream.

- **Don't feel guilty.** You are giving an enormous amount of attention and love to your baby. You don't need to feel guilty for giving a little attention and love to the person with whom you chose to become a parent.

- **Do be nice.** Be sure to acknowledge all the things that your partner is doing well. It's too easy to complain and criticize instead of remembering that it's challenging for the both of you.

Trust Yourself

Follow your mothering instincts. They are strong and typically right on! You don't have to listen to all of the advice given by your family, friends, or "experts" (that includes us!) if it doesn't feel right for you. Remember that you know your baby better than anyone.

TOP TEN TIPS FOR BECOMING A MOTHER WITHOUT LOSING YOURSELF

Over time we have tried to capture the heart of our process in a series of easy to remember tips for busy mothers. We have included them here as well as our thoughts on each tip and ideas on how to practice them. These tips are useful now and even more so after your baby arrives. Enjoy and share these with every new mother you know!

1. Let go of half the stuff you are trying to do.
2. Don't waste time with limiting beliefs
3. Always ask *how* you can get what you need, not why you can't.
4. If you want something to happen, schedule it.
5. Remember that taking care of yourself has EVERYTHING to do with being a good mother.
6. Stop to self-reflect . . . often.
7. Decide what is non-negotiable in your life and stop negotiating with yourself and others.
8. Act! Take one step towards what you want *today*.
9. Live your values.
10. Make your own rules.

1. Let Go of Half the Stuff You Are Trying to Do.

Okay, let's be blunt. After your baby arrives, chances are you will never be able to do everything you feel compelled to put on your task list. The women we know who try to juggle it all, maintaining everything from their pre-baby life plus all the new roles and responsibilities associated with motherhood, usually end up stressed out, exhausted, and resentful. With good reason, it's TOO much to do.

If you want to be a mother without losing yourself, you need to let go of a huge chunk of what you are trying to do. It's vital that you have the energy, space, and time to BE there in your life. Time to learn your new role. Space to shift and change. Energy to see solutions not problems. You will not stay true to who you really are if you spend all your time working through a list of tasks a mile long.

The sad thing is that more often than not, it's you who will be putting the pressure and expectations on yourself. We want to help relieve the pressure right now. You have our permission to let go of half the stuff you are trying to do. Not only today but in the future, when you get caught up in the busy-ness of your new life and forget that it doesn't need to be so hard.

> *"It's remarkable how caught up in the doing I get. I always feel like there is no possible way I can cut my list. I think I secretly believe my value as a 'mom' comes from doing a lot, being really busy. And yet, every time I push to pare down my list, the rewards are immediate. My stress drops. The feeling that I can never catch up goes away. I slow down and start to really enjoy my life and my baby again."*
> —*LACEY*

QUICK FIX

Make a list of everything that's on your plate right now and cross off half of it, just to see what it feels like. Think of it as an experiment. Take the perspective that you are letting go of some of your tasks "for now." Live with and use the short list for one week. At the end of the week, notice how you feel, what was different in the past week, and if you really need to add back the tasks you cut.

2. Don't Waste Time with Limiting Beliefs.

We've already discussed the importance of choosing your beliefs about motherhood and the difference between empowering and limiting beliefs, but we can't stress enough that limiting beliefs are a waste of time. In the midst of new motherhood, those limiting beliefs that you eliminated earlier in *Becoming a Mother* can try and creep back and regain their hold on your life. The nature of new motherhood—lack of sleep, lots to do and learn, and the shocking realization of the power and responsibility you have—can leave you feeling vulnerable. It becomes easy for doubt and negativity to resurface.

It's up to you to be vigilant and protect your new life and its possibilities, choosing again and again what you want to believe. For example, the first time something doesn't go the way you hoped with your baby and you notice yourself thinking, "I'm not a very good mother"—toss that encroaching limiting belief out the window! Quickly say out loud, "I'm a great mother." What you think is what begins to create your reality.

Just remember, don't waste your precious time with limiting beliefs—yours or anyone else's.

> "The limiting belief that always gets me is 'I'm not as good as other mothers.' It usually tries to ambush me when I'm with a group of moms and their babies — I find myself comparing my baby to theirs, my way of parenting to theirs, etc. Here is my new empowering belief, 'There are many wonderful ways to mother and my way is best for us.' It is helping already!"   —JOAN

QUICK FIX

When you are feeling like those limiting beliefs are crowding in around you, stop. Take a piece of paper and write down the limiting belief or negative thought that is bringing you down. Cross it out and write down the opposite belief or thought. Put the piece of paper in your pocket and refer to as necessary!

3. Always Ask *How* You Can Get What You Need, Not Why You Can't.

As a new mother, you are going to need a lot of things—a never-ending stream of gear as your baby rapidly grows and changes, new skills, friends who are also new moms, babysitters, emotional support, physical support, help with cleaning, pats on the back. To get what you need quickly and easily, remember that it's all available to you. You just have to learn to ask.

This is about being solution oriented. You can spend your time thinking about why you can't get what you need—"It's too much to ask," "They are too busy," "I should be able to do this by myself." Or you can spend your time strategizing on *how* you can get what you need. Put your energy into the solution, use the tools that you learned in this book, and always go after what you need and want with confidence.

> *"This is my favorite tip. I've watched a lot of new moms get whiny or turn into mother martyrs. They talk about how they need more sleep or help or understanding from their partners but never seem to do anything about it. I just march up to my husband and say, 'I really need more sleep today. How can we make that happen?' It totally works."*   —TONI

QUICK FIX

Get into the habit of asking how you can get what you need. Instead of complaining, wishing, or hinting around for something, simply ask out loud, "How can I get _____?" Whether you are asking yourself or someone else, say it just like that. We guarantee you will move toward a solution.

4. If You Want Something to Happen, Schedule It.

Life can move pretty quickly when you are a mom, especially after the first few months when the cocoon-like world of brand new motherhood shifts into the busy world of day-to-day motherhood. The hours, days, and weeks start to slip by faster than you could have imagined. Along with them can slip away some of your important intentions.

It's easy to think about the things you want to do but never actually get around to doing them, especially those close-to-the-heart things like sitting down and adding to your baby's scrapbook, having a date night with your partner, or getting the massage you promised yourself.

Don't let your good intentions go to waste. If you want something to happen, schedule it! Use the modeling techniques that you learned in this book. Get out your calendar and schedule in your top priorities. Make sure to be realistic about what it will take to follow through. Consider whether you'll need a babysitter, don't overbook yourself, and plan ahead.

> *"I didn't use this tip for the first eight months as a new mother. I had twins and was plowing forward with my head down, doing the best I could. At some point, I looked back at my notes from Becoming a Mother and remembered how I promised myself that by six months, my partner and I would do a mini getaway — a romantic dinner, maybe even spend a night in a hotel. By eight months, we desperately needed some time together but it seemed impossible. I thought about this tip and sat down with my partner and circled a day on the calendar. That got us brainstorming on some ideas and two weeks later we ended up at our favorite Italian restaurant with my mother and sister manning the fort. Success!"* —EILEEN

QUICK FIX

Make scheduling a habit. Pick a recurring period of time — monthly works well for most new mothers — to stop and schedule those things that will make your life fulfilling. Put a big reminder on your calendar or ask someone to remind you to actually *do* the scheduling!

5. Remember That Taking Care of Yourself Has EVERYTHING to Do with Being a Good Mother.

As a new mother, don't fall into the trap of thinking that it is okay if you come last. It isn't. You need to be available for your baby and your family; you need to be energized and whole; you need to feel fulfilled and complete so that you can *give* to the people you love.

Anyone who's ever flown on an airplane knows that adults need to put on their oxygen masks before they put on their child's. If you do not have your own capacity, you cannot take care of those who depend on you.

It is your responsibility to ensure that you are okay; that you are rested and healthy; that you are eating well, exercising, getting out, interacting with friends and loved ones, laughing, and generally taking good care of yourself. This is the foundation you need to be a good mother, to give your best to your child, and to be able to sustain the long term commitment that is motherhood

> *"I love passing this tip on to other new mothers. It's a lovely reminder that being a good mother doesn't come from beating yourself up or self-sacrificing to the point of exhaustion or illness. We mothers are important! We have a huge job and need to give ourselves every opportunity to do it well."*   —SHARON

QUICK FIX

What is your "oxygen mask?" What are the things that keep you "breathing" so that you can take care of the ones you love? Narrow it down to the absolute essentials, then share them with your loved ones. Use the rest of the tips — asking how you can get what you need, scheduling what's important to you — to be sure that you have everything to take care of yourself so that you can take care of everyone else.

6. Stop to Self-Reflect . . . Often.

Time and the ability to self-reflect is a must-have as a new mother. It's the often overlooked key to keeping your head straight. If you never stop to see where you are, what you've learned so far, and where you want to go, you can end up running around in circles, frazzled and reactive. The busy pace and ever changing nature of new motherhood is best managed by frequent adjustment, proactive thinking, creative solutions, and a calm and clear mind. All of that comes from quiet self-reflection.

Self-reflection doesn't have to be fancy or take a long time—you can just stop, breathe, and take two minutes to check in on how you are feeling and doing. Or, you can treat yourself to the luxury of some more relaxed time to yourself. Stopping for ten minutes, a half hour, or an hour to journal or think can work wonders.

There are many moments as a new mother that are perfectly designed for self-reflection—feeding your baby, taking your baby out for a stroll, and rocking your baby are all activities that lend themselves well to quiet thought. The trick is to re-member to *use* one of those moments for reflection. You now have many different ways to remind yourself to follow through on the things that are important to you. Make sure that reflection is one of them.

> *"I wish someone had encouraged me to stop and think when I had my first baby! I ran around going from task to task — sleep deprived and doing the opposite of self-reflection, it was more like self-denial. The second time around I learned the value of slowing down to ask myself questions, notice what I was feeling, and really listen to myself. It made a huge difference in how I connected with my children and how I felt about me."*   —CLAIRE

QUICK FIX

If you find that your good intentions to self-reflect never seem to actually happen, try writing down three questions on a piece of paper to help get things started. Create your own or feel free to use any of the questions below. Make copies of the questions and use them as worksheets—just scribble the date on top and any thoughts generated by the questions. Use as frequently as needed!

What's working well?
What would make things easier?
What am I loving?
What is draining me?
What do I really need from my husband/partner?
What's most important for the next day/week?
How can I take better care of myself?
What would I like to see change?

7. Decide What Is Non-Negotiable in Your Life and Stop Negotiating with Yourself and Others.

Sometimes you have to be firm as a mother. Now's the time to start practicing—on yourself! You deserve and require certain things for your life that are absolutely necessary—you needn't second-guess yourself nor let others question it.

What are important non-negotiables? Some are no-brainers—sleep, healthy food, water, a shower or a bath. Others depend entirely on the individual—one new mother's "must have" might be time to play the piano, someone else might require shared cooking duty with her partner, or someone else a chance for coffee with her best girlfriend.

Only you can decide what are the must-haves and then make no apologies or excuses about making it your priority.

You've thought a lot about what you want for your new life and how you want to experience motherhood. Give some attention to determining what it is that is truly non-negotiable and make it happen.

> *"My non-negotiable in the first month of new motherhood was attending my cousin's wedding in Hawaii. We knew there would be challenges, but there would be grandparents coming who might not be around much longer. I felt this was something I needed to do, no matter how crazy it seemed. I have no regrets. I think we made it work because I had such a strong conviction that it had to happen."* —RITA

QUICK FIX

Pick one non-negotiable this week. It might be something basic (food, water, sleep), or it might be something that goes more to the heart of who you are. Communicate it. Talk to your partner or whoever else is involved, and let him or her know how important it is to you. Ask for support in making it happen.

8. Act! Take One Step Toward What You Want Today.

We emphasized the power and impact of taking action as one of the last steps in *Becoming a Mother*. After your baby arrives, it continues to be crucial to turn desire into action.

New motherhood can be overwhelming—in the first few weeks, just taking a bath and remembering to brush your teeth can feel like a monumental achievement. Somehow in the whirl of new motherhood, a woman can forget that she is powerful, that she can make anything happen by taking one step at a time. All goals are easier when you break them down—usually you just need to figure out what the next step is.

Whether it is working toward your baby sleeping through the night, starting to exercise, or creating space for romance in your relationship, identifying just one step to take *today* keeps things simple—no matter how complicated they may seem in the moment.

> *"During my first year as a new mom, I often felt overwhelmed by the seeming enormity of certain tasks. Like childproofing. When Ian started to crawl, I couldn't see how we could possibly create a safe environment for him short of getting rid of all of our furniture. Finally, I tried to simplify and figured something was better than nothing. I went out and bought some cheap foam mattress covers and taped them around the more dangerous furniture. That one action relieved a great deal of my anxiety and got me started on the bigger job."* —BARBARA

QUICK FIX

Identify what it is that's overwhelming you. You do not need to know how to fix it; you do not need to know all the steps. Just choose one thing that you can do to take action on it. Later, take another step and another. Allow yourself to *not know* everything but to take action nonetheless.

9. Live Your Values.

As you already know from reading this book, your values are an essential part of who you are and how you experience motherhood. This tip is just a reminder of how important those values are—and to live as closely as you can to them everyday.

Use your "My Foundation for Motherhood" to help you keep your values present and top of mind. You need to remind yourself what your values are so that you can bring them into your life as a new mother. This is your opportunity to create a life around what truly fulfills you.

Remember, your values can help bring fulfillment to every aspect of your life. They can assist you in determining your approach to each challenge of new motherhood, who you choose to surround yourself with, how to spend your day, and even what thoughts to focus on.

Living your values is all about being conscious and letting what really matters drive your life.

> *"Identifying my values was such an eye-opener for me. It really let me align my life with what I cared about and let go the rest. I decided to actually memorize my values so they are with me every moment. It's funny now how I can be sitting in traffic, irritable and rushed, when my one of my values will pop into my head and remind me of how I really want to be!"*   —LYNDA

QUICK FIX

Do a sanity check on how you are living your values. Take out your "My Foundation for Motherhood" and quickly rate how well you are living each value on a scale of one to ten. Circle the value with the lowest score and make that the "value of the day." Look for ways to honor that value in every aspect of your life just for the day!

10. Make Your Own Rules.

It's your life! Make your own rules. Be a new mom on *your* terms. You have something unique to offer the sisterhood of motherhood. Bring your creativity, special gifts, and perspective on the world. If you don't like the parenting techniques you have been reading about—create your own! Not too keen on the mommies' groups you have been attending? Start a new group! Don't like the childcare options you are finding? Brainstorm with like-minded mothers and try a new approach.

We know a lot of mothers who have changed their corner of the world this way, from women who have changed the rules of their employers to include flex time and daycare, to women who have decided to be breadwinners while their husbands became stay-at-home dads, to women who have arranged co-ops of free childcare. Everything is possible.

Whatever you do, don't settle. Don't compromise. Make motherhood work for you.

"I felt so pressured by motherhood—everybody was so sure about what I should be doing except me! I finally realized that I could do it my way, and that my way was the best way of all!" —PAULA

QUICK FIX

Be attuned to the things that aren't working for you, and ask yourself, "If I had it my way, how would it be?" Then make up your own rules and see if it can be that way, after all.

WE'RE HERE TO HELP YOU!

At Empowered Motherhood[LLC] we are always available to answer your questions, hear your stories, take your suggestions, celebrate your accomplishments, and assist you on your journey of becoming a mother without losing yourself. We are here to help you while you are expecting your baby AND to fully support you afterwards in your years as an amazing woman and mother!

Contact us for any or all of the following:

- **Free Kit.** Sign up on our website to get your free Moving Into Motherhood Kit and our marvelous newsletter—a weekly boost for moms-to-be.

- **Extra Resources.** Don't miss all the free extras including the electronic versions of the *Becoming a Mother* worksheets and special bonus tools for our readers. Sign up on our website!

- **Self-Coaching Tools.** Browse through our shopping cart of tools to help you balance career, motherhood, and self, including e-books, worksheets, and digital audio recordings that you use to coach yourself.

- **Virtual Seminar.** Join our intimate and personalized virtual seminars where you work with a coach and other empowered moms-to-be in weekly group calls taking you through the *Becoming a Mother* process step by step.

- **Personal Coaching.** Hire your very own personal coach dedicated to accelerating your *Becoming a Mother* process and bringing out your full potential as a woman and mother.

- **New Mom Support.** Explore our ever-growing list of services and products that help you access your full potential after your baby arrives.
- **Feedback.** Tell us what you need and want as a woman and mother. Help us grow our company and empower women around the world!

Empowered MotherhoodLLC
info@empoweredmotherhood.com
www.empoweredmotherhood.com
*special code: fabulous